Making Words
Kindergarten

Making Words Kindergarten

50 Interactive Lessons that Build Phonemic Awareness, Phonics, and Spelling Skills

Dorothy P. Hall

Wake Forest University

Patricia M. Cunningham

Wake Forest University

PEARSON

Boston • New York • San Francisco
Mexico City • Montreal • Toronto • London • Madrid • Munich • Paris
Hong Kong • Singapore • Tokyo • Cape Town • Sydney

Executive Editor: Aurora Martínez Ramos
Series Editorial Assistant: Kara Kikel
Director of Professional Development: Alison Maloney
Marketing Manager: Danae April
Production Editor: Annette Joseph
Editorial Production Service: Lynda Griffiths
Composition Buyer: Linda Cox
Manufacturing Buyer: Linda Morris
Electronic Composition: Denise Hoffman
Interior Design: Denise Hoffman
Cover Administrator: Kristina Mose-Libon

For related titles and support materials, visit our online catalog at www.ablongman.com.

Between the time website information is gathered and then published, it is not unusual for some sites to have closed. Also, the transcription of URLs can result in typographical errors. The publisher would appreciate notification where these errors occur so that they may be corrected in subsequent editions.

ISBN-10: 0-205-58096-3
ISBN-13: 978-0-205-58096-5

Printed in the United States of America

10 9 8 7 6 5   11

Photos: Dorothy P. Hall.

About the Authors

Pat   Dottie

Dorothy P. Hall

I always wanted to teach young children. After graduating from Worcester State College in Massachusetts, I taught first and second grades. Two years later, I moved to North Carolina, where I continued teaching in the primary grades. Many children I worked with in the newly integrated schools struggled in learning to read. Wanting to increase my knowledge, I received my M.Ed. and Ed.D. in Reading from the University of North Carolina at Greensboro. I also worked at Wake Forest University, where I met and began to work with Pat Cunningham.

After three years of teaching at the college level I returned to the public schools and taught third and fourth grades and served as a reading and curriculum coordinator for my school district. At this time Pat Cunningham and I began to collaborate on a number of projects. In 1989, we developed the Four Blocks Framework, a comprehensive approach to literacy in grades 1, 2, and 3, which we called Big Blocks. Later, we expanded the program to include kindergarten, calling it Building Blocks. By 1999, Pat and I had written four *Making Words* books, a series of *Month by Month Phonics* books, and *The Teacher's Guide to Four Blocks*, and I retired from the school system to devote more time to consulting and writing. I also went back to work at Wake Forest University, where I taught courses in reading, children's literature, and language arts instruction for elementary education students.

Today, I am Director of the Four Blocks Center at Wake Forest University and enjoy working with teachers and administrators around the country presenting workshops on Four Blocks, Building Blocks, guided reading strategies, and phonics instruction. I have also written several books with teachers. One request Pat and I have had for a number of years is to revise the *Making Words* by grade level and include a scope and sequence for the phonics instruction taught. Here it is—Enjoy!

Patricia M. Cunningham

From the day I entered first grade, I knew I wanted to be a first-grade teacher. In 1965, I graduated from the University of Rhode Island and began my teaching career teaching first grade in Key West, Florida. For the next several years, I taught a variety of grades and worked as a curriculum coordinator and special reading teacher in Florida and Indiana. From the very beginning, I worried about the children who struggled in learning to read and so I devised a variety of alternative strategies to teach them to read. In 1974, I received my Ph.D. in Reading Education from the University of Georgia.

I developed the Making Words activity while working with Title I teachers in North Carolina, where I was the Director of Reading for Alamance County Schools. I have been the Director of Elementary Education at Wake Forest University in Winston-Salem, North Carolina, since 1980 and have worked with numerous teachers to develop hands-on, engaging ways to teach phonics and spelling. In 1991, I wrote *Phonics They Use: Words for Reading and Writing*, which is currently available in its fourth edition. Along with Richard Allington, I also wrote *Classrooms that Work* and *Schools that Work*.

Dottie Hall and I have worked together on many projects. In 1989, we began developing the Four Blocks Framework, a comprehensive approach to literacy that is used in many schools in the United States and Canada. Dottie and I have produced many books together, including the first *Making Words* books and the *Month by Month Phonics* books. These *Making Words* for grade levels kindergarten to fifth grade are in response to requests by teachers across the years to have Making Words lessons with a scope and sequence tailored to their various grade levels. We hope you and your students will enjoy these Making Words lessons and we would love to hear your comments and suggestions.

Contents

Introduction

Language learning is an active process that begins at birth and continues throughout life. *Phonological awareness* and *phonemic awareness* are terms that refer to children's understandings about words and sounds in words. Phonological awareness is broader in scope and includes the ability to separate sentences into words and words into syllables. Phonemic awareness includes the ability to recognize that words are made up of a discrete set of sounds and the ability to manipulate sounds. Phonemic awareness is an oral ability—the ability to hear that words begin alike, that words rhyme, and that, for example, there are three sounds in the word **c-a-t**. Both phonological awareness and phonemic awareness are highly correlated with success in beginning reading (Adams, 1990; Griffith & Olson, 1992; Yopp, 1995; Ehri & Nunes, 2002; National Reading Panel, 2000; Cunningham, 2005). Phonics instruction begins with learning to tie particular consonant letters to the sounds they typically make. Unlike phonemic awareness, which requires students to pay attention to sound only, learning a letter sound requires students to attend to both the visual form of the letter and the sound it makes. Phonics knowledge is necessary to read or decode unknown words and to spell or encode words.

Making Words (Cunningham, 1991; Cunningham & Hall, 1994, 1997; Cunningham & Cunningham, 1992) is a multilevel phonics and spelling activity in elementary schools in which students are given a certain number of letter cards and asked to manipulate these letter cards to make words. In this active, hands-on, manipulative activity, children discover letter-sound relationships and learn how to look for patterns in words. During Making Words lessons, children also learn that changing one letter changes the word to another word. This instruction can begin in kindergarten. Teachers can help young students blend letter sounds together to make a word, then segment or take off a letter and change the beginning letter(s) to make new words with the same spelling pattern or word family.

In kindergarten classes, or in classes of emergent second-language learners or children with special needs, Making Words instruction should *not* start at the beginning of the school year. It is best to begin after all the letters have been introduced and reviewed with a class activity such as "Getting to Know You" (Cunningham, 2005; Hall & Cunningham, 2003; Hall & Williams, 2000). Also, students do *not* use the individual little letter cards in kindergarten as is done in the other grade levels. Instead, children use a *class set of yarned letter cards*. The letters are written in black on white cardboard or tagboard, capitals on one side and lowercase letters on the other side with yarn attached to the top. Children wear these yarned letter cards around their necks and become the letters they are wearing and make words using just one pattern or "word family."

Making Yarned Letter Cards

Copy or cut out the large black letters provided in the back of this book onto 9 × 12-inch white construction paper or tagboard. Remember to put the capital letters on one side and the lowercase letters on the other side. Laminate these letter cards so they can be reused. Finally, punch two holes at the top to create "letter necklaces" to go around your students' necks. Make sure the letters have lowercase on one side and capital letters on the other side because you will need capital letters to make names. (Patterns for these 26 letter cards with capital and small letters are in the back of the book.) You will need a few extra letter cards for some lessons that have more than one of the same letters in them (such as **e, b, l, n, p,** and **t**).

Steps for a Making Words Lesson in Kindergarten

This lesson will take perhaps 30 minutes the first few times, but as the students get used to the procedure it will take less time.

Here are the steps of the Making Words lesson in a kindergarten class:

1. **Read a book to the class.** This step is important for transfer. One source of books, each book with many words using one spelling pattern or phonogram, is Fred's Phonograms. This series was published in 2001 by I Knew That, Inc., in Seattle, Washington (www.iknewthatinc.com). These small books are filled with words using the spelling pattern you will be working with that day and can be used to start these lessons. Some of the titles are *Stan's Plan, The Black Shack, Pop's Shop, The Same Name,* and *Stay and Play.* Many teachers, however, prefer to read trade books instead so we have listed some books with the rhymes for each lesson. The Dr. Seuss books contain many of the rhyming words or spelling patterns you will be working on and are easy to find at your school or local library as well as most bookstores that sell children's books. Nonfiction is a popular choice for books with many young children, so if you have a book about snakes (**ake**), frogs (**og**), cats (**at**), or dogs (**og**), think about reading or rereading that book the day you are working on that pattern. After reading the book, **point out a spelling pattern** or word family in the book and talk about the pattern.

2. **Make words, blend the letter sounds together, and read the words made by the children wearing yarned letter cards.** Have the children wearing the yarned letter cards for the letters in a particular pattern come stand in front of the class. The children wearing letter cards with letters that are *not* in the pattern stand *with* the pattern and make words. The teacher and the children blend the letter sounds together and then the teacher uses each new word in a sentence. When a name is made, the teacher talks about the name and how the children will need to turn their letter card around to the capital letter side. To make the lesson

more multilevel, include words in which your students need to blend two initial consonants to read and spell the words (**bl**, **br**, **cl**, **cr**, **dr**, **fl**, **fr**, **gr**, **pl**, **pr**, **sk**, **sl**, **sm**, **sn**, **sp**, **st**, and **tr**). If the letter sounds for **ch**, **th**, and **sh** have been taught, use these to make words also. Be sure the words you make are known by most of the students in your class. Sometimes there are more words we can make with blends but we would have to add more letter card children to the front of the class, so we do not make them.

3. Spell and make words by segmenting and blending beginning sounds with the pattern. The teacher has the children wearing the letter cards for this particular pattern continue to stand in front of the class. Then, the teacher asks what letter is needed to spell a word. The children are asked to point to the child wearing the appropriate letter card and that letter child comes and stands with the letter card children in the pattern. As the teacher says each word, the children are asked to point to these letters (or onsets) that together with the spelling pattern (rime) can make words.

4. Collect the letter cards. Call for each of the letters. This is a quick review of letter names for children who still need this practice.

An Example of Making Words in Kindergarten

Pattern: at

Letter cards needed for this lesson: a, t, b, c, f, h, l, m, p, r, and s

1. Read a book to the class. After reading a rhyming book, such as Dr. Seuss's *Cat in the Hat*, or a nonfiction book about cats, the teacher would talk about the rhyming words **cat** and **hat** or just the word **cat** and let two children put on the yarned letter cards and become the letters **a** and **t**.

The teacher then passes out several other yarned letter cards (**b**, **c**, **f**, **h**, **l**, **m**, **p**, **r**, and **s**) to other children in the class. These cards have the beginning consonants on them that will make words with the **at** pattern.

2. Making Words: Blend and segment letter sounds to read words. Standing in front of the class, the teacher sees that the children with the letter cards **a** and **t** are standing together; she or he may even ask the two children with the letters **a** and **t** to hold hands or put their arms around each other. Then the teacher, along with the students, will blend these two letter sounds together and say **a/t**. The teacher asks the **c** to join **a** and **t** and then asks the children the word they have just made. If someone knows the word is **cat**, the teacher and the class blend together the letter sounds **c/a/t** and say **cat**.

If no one knows, then the teacher leads the class to blend these three letter sounds together and say **c/a/t**, **cat**. Next, the teacher uses the word **cat** in a sentence: "I once had a big, fat, gray **cat**." Then the teacher has another letter child **b** stand in front of the letters **a** and **t** and asks, "Who can read the word I just made?" Together the teacher and the class blend the three letter sounds to make another word, **b/a/t**, **bat**. Again, he or she uses the word in a sentence: "I hit the ball with a **bat**." The teacher continues like this with the letters **f**, **h**, **m**, **p**, **r**, and **s** (**f/a/t**, **fat**; **h/a/t**, **hat**; **m/a/t**, **mat**; **p/a/t**, **pat**, **Pat**; **r/a/t**, **rat**; and **s/a/t**, **sat**). If a name can be made with the pattern, the teacher talks about names and how if they make the name **Pat**, they will need to turn their letter card around to the capital letter side.

"Names, just like your name, need a capital letter at the beginning."

To make the lesson more multi-level, have two children come to the front of the class together and blend these two beginning letter sounds, or the onset, and read and spell words that begin with two letter sounds such as **brat** and **flat**. If you have already taught the **ch** and **th** sounds to your class, then you can make and read **chat** and **that**.

3. Making Words: Blend and segment letter sounds to spell words. Next, the children do another round of Making Words using the letter cards, this time not only blending and segmenting (taking away) sounds but also listening for what letter they need to make or *spell* a word. Once again, the teacher stands in front of the class or group and has the letters **a** and **t** stand together; she or he may ask those two children to hold hands or put their arms around each other. The teacher blends these two letter sounds together and leads the class to say **at**. Next, the teacher says a word that can be made by adding a letter to **at**, such as **cat**. She or he asks all the children in the class to point to the letter needed to make the word **cat**. The children point to **c** and the teacher asks **c** to come and stand with **at** and leads the class to say **cat, c/at**. He or she has **c** leave (segmenting) and **at** is left standing alone. They then use this **at** pattern to do a second round of Making Words, asking, "What letter do we need to make (spell) **bat**? **fat**? **mat**? **rat**? **sat**? **pat**? **Pat**? **flat**? **brat**? (**chat**? **that**?) For each word, the class will be asked to point to and name the letter that should stand next to **at** to spell the word. The child wearing the needed letter will join the two **at** children and hold his or her letter card (**b, f, h, m, r, s,** or **P**) in front of **at** to spell or make each of the words. If someone makes a name, the teacher talks about how that child will need to turn his or her letter card around to the capital letter side.

Introduction

4. Collect the letter cards by calling for each of the letters. When the children have made words with the **at** pattern and have read and spelled the words with the teacher, she or he then collects the letter cards by saying, "Will the person who has the **a** bring it to me. Will the person with the letter **t** bring it to me," continuing in any order until all the letter cards are collected by the teacher. This will help the students who still need practice with letter names.

The manipulation of letters and sounds to make new words is an important part of learning to read, and making words is a wonderful way to introduce your kindergarten class to the concept now known as "onset and rhyme." Young children understand things they can *see*, and wearing the letters and "making words" is an excellent way for children to "see" how beginning sounds and spelling patterns come together to make many different words. We want children to see that there is a system and a pattern in the way letters represent sounds, and that is why we try pointing out these "patterns" in our instruction. When young children see a new word, we want them to ask themselves how this word is like other words they know, so they can discover patterns on their own. Making Words helps children see patterns in words, and in this book we have adapted the activity for the youngest learners in elementary school: kindergarten students.

Making Words—Another Example with Three Letters and Two Sounds in the Pattern

Pattern: **ack**

Letter cards needed for this lesson: **a, c, k, b, j, l, m, p, r, s, t**, and **z**.

1. Read a book to the class. After reading the rhyming text of the book *Zoo Looking*, by Mem Fox, you can extend this activity and work on phonemic awareness, phonics, and spelling with your students with this Making Words activity appropriate for kindergarten. Using the 9 × 12-inch white construction paper or tagboard letter, choose three students (one for **a**, one for **c**, and one for **k**) and have them stand together to make the **ack** spelling pattern or word family. Explain to the class that **c** and **k** make the same sound and just one sound is heard for those two letters. Together, the teacher and the class blend the two sounds together and say **a/ck, ack**. Other children are given letter cards and become the beginning letters **b, j, l, m, p, r, s, t**, and **z**.

2. Making Words: Blend and segment letter sounds to read words. Let **b** stand with **a**, **c**, and **k** in front of the class. Together, the teacher and the class blend the letters and say **b/a/ck**, then the word **back**. Then the teacher uses the word **back** in a sentence: "Go to the **back** of the line." Take away (segment) the **b** and say what is left—**ack**. Then have the other letters come up one at a time and stand with the letters **ack**. Make sure the new letter stands in front of, or right before, the letters **a-c-k**.

Ask who can read the new words as the children (who are wearing the other letter cards) come to the front and join **ack** to make a new word: **J/a/ck**, **Jack**; **M/a/ck**, **Mack**; **p/a/ck**, **pack**; **r/a/ck**, **rack**; **s/a/ck**, **sack**; **t/a/ck**, **tack**; and **Z/a/ck**, **Zack**. If a name can be made with the pattern, the teacher may talk about names and how if the children make the name **Jack**, **Mack**, or **Zack** they will need to turn their letter card around to the capital letter side. "Names, just like your name, need a capital letter at the beginning."

To end the making of words, the teacher can make the lesson more multilevel by having two children come up together and blend the sounds on their letter cards together to make the beginning sounds, or onsets, and make words that begin with two letter sounds such as **black**, **track**, and **smack**. (If you have taught your students the sound for the letters **sh**, then make the word **shack** also.)

3. Making Words: Blend and segment letter sounds to spell words. For this second round of the Making Words lesson we blend and segment letters to spell the words we are making. First, we start with three children wearing letter cards again (one child to be the letter **a**, another for **c**, and another for **k**). These three children become the **ack** spelling pattern or word family. Other children will become the consonants: **b**, **j**, **l**, **m**, **p**, **r**, **s**, **t**, and **z**. The teacher says, "I want to make the word **back**. What letter do I need with **ack** to make **back**?" The children are asked to point to the letter and then the letter **b** stands with **a**, **c**, and **k** in front of the class. Together, the teacher and the class blend the letters and sounds together and say **b-ack** then the word **back**. Take away (segment) the **b** and say what is left—**ack**. Ask, "What letter do I need to make the name **Jack**?" The children point to the **j** and that letter comes up and stands with the letters **ack**. Together, everyone spells and says the new word as children (who are wearing the other letters) come to the front and join **ack** to become new words. Each time they make a name, the teacher talks about how if they make a word that is a name, like **Jack**, they will need to turn their letter card around to the capital letter side. "Names, just like your name, need a capital letter at the beginning." Continue to spell some other words with this **ack** pattern: **Mack**, **pack**, **rack**, **sack**, **tack**, **Zack**, **black**, **track** (**shack**).

4. Collect the letter cards by calling for each of the letters. When the children have made words with the **ack** pattern and have read and spelled the words with the teacher, she or he then collects the letter cards by saying, "Will the person who has the **a** bring it to me. Will the person with the letter **c** bring it to me," continuing in any order until all the letter cards are collected from the students. This collecting activity will help those students who still need practice with letter names.

Making Words–Another Example with Silent Vowel Sounds

Pattern: **ake**

Letter needed: **a**, **e**, **k**, **b**, **c**, **f**, **j**, **l**, **m**, **r**, **t**, and **w**

1. Read a book to the class. *Jake Baked the Cake* by B. G. Hennessy (Puffin Books, 1992). Read the book, then have the children listen as you reread the refrain on any of several pages, "While *Jake* b*ake*d the c*ake*." Talk about the **ake** pattern and sound. If you can't find this book, there are two others you could use. One is *Hunky Dory Ate It* by Katie Evans (Puffin Unicorn Books, 1992). Read the book and then reread the first two sentences in the book, "Clara **Lake baked** a **cake**. Hunky Dory Ate It!" and have the children listen for the **ake** pattern in **Lake**, **baked**, and **cake**. The other possibility is *I Can Read with My Eyes Shut!* by Dr. Seuss (Random House, 1978). Read the book, then reread page 19 and talk about the **ake** pattern in **Jake** and **Snake**. Or read any nonfiction book about snakes and talk about the **ake** sound in **snake**.

2. Making Words: Blend and segment letter sounds to read words. Using the three letter cards, **a**, **k**, and **e**, worn by three different children, the teacher has them stand in front of the class. The teacher then explains to the children that they can hear only the **a** and **k** in this pattern, but not the **e**. Have the child wearing the letter card **e** put his hand over his mouth and explain to the children the **e** is silent and says nothing in this pattern. Tell the students, "We call this a silent **e**."

Other children are given big letter cards and become the letters **b**, **c**, **f**, **j**, **l**, **m**, **r**, **t**, and **w**. The letter card children **ake** may be asked to hold hands or put their arms around each other to show they belong together.

The teacher puts the child with the letter card **c** in front of **ake** and asks the children to read the word she or he made. The teacher leads the class to say **c** and then **ake** and finally the word **cake**. She or he then uses the word in a sentence: "I like to bake a **cake** for special days, like birthdays or holidays."

Next, the teacher makes and reads some other words: **b/ake**, **bake**; **f/ake**, **fake**; **J/ake**, **Jake**; **m/ake**, **make**; **l/ake**, **lake**; **r/ake**, **rake**; **t/ake**, **take**; and **w/ake**, **wake**. When a name is made, the teacher talks about the name and how the children will need to turn their letter card around to the capital letter side. The teacher can make the lesson more multilevel by having two children come up together and blend the sounds on their letter cards together to make the beginning sounds, or onset, and make and read the words that begin with two letter sounds, such as the name **Blake** or the words **flake** and **brake**. (If you have already taught the **sh** sound then make the word **shake**.)

3. Making Words: Blend and segment letter sounds to spell words. Using the three letter cards, **a**, **k**, and **e**, the teacher and class say **ake**. The teacher then asks the children to point to the letter that will make the word **bake**. When they point to the letter **b**, she or he leads the class to say **b-ake**, **bake**. The teacher then follows the same procedure to spell the word **cake**, asking, "What letter do we need to make the **cake**?" When the children point to the letter **c** the teacher leads them to say **c** and **ake**, and **cake**, continuing on with **fake**, **Jake**, **make**, **lake**, **rake**, **take**, and **wake**, and **Blake**, **brake**, **sake (shake)**.

4. Collect the letter cards by calling for each of the letters. When the children have made words with the **ake** pattern and have read and spelled the words with the teacher, she or he collects the letter cards by saying, "Will the person who has the **a** bring it to me. Will the person with the letter card **k** bring it to me," continuing in any order until all the letter cards are collected from the students.

Review Lessons

After approximately every five lessons we have placed a review lesson.

1. Line up the needed letter card children. For review lessons simply have the children who are wearing the letter cards listed at the top of the review lesson page stand in front of the class.

2. Choose three or four letter card children and make a word. Ask the class to read the word. *For this review activity have the children give you a sentence using the word.* Continue this way until you have made and the children have read all 10 words.

3. Next, ask the class what letters are needed to spell each of the 10 words one at a time. Together you and the children stretch out the word, listening for letter sounds in each word. The children tell you what letters they need to spell the word.

The words are ordered so that just one letter card child needs to move back and another move up in front to make or spell most words in the lesson. This order helps the lesson flow more easily and lets the children see how changing just one letter may make a new word. Sometimes two letters need to move but never will all of the letter card children need to move.

Spelling Patterns and How to Use Them

Rhyming patterns (high-utility phonograms from Wylie and Durrell, 1970) or word families you can use include **ack**, **ail**, **ain**, **ake**, **am**, **ame**, **an**, **ank**, **ap**, **ash**, **at**, **ate**, **aw**, **ay**, **eat**, **ell**, **est**, **ice**, **ick**, **ide**, **ight**, **ill**, **in**, **ine**, **ing**, **ink**, **ip**, **it**, **ock**, **oke**, **op**, **ore**, **ot**, **uck**, **ug**, **ump**, and **unk**. We have found it best to start with those easiest to explain to young children. Those are the spelling patterns where the letter sounds are simply blended together (for example, **a** and **t** make the **at** pattern and **o** and **p** to make **op** pattern). Later we explain that sometimes two letters have just one sound (such as **a** and **ck** or **e** and **ll**). This is followed by talking about more difficult patterns such as the silent **e** on the end of a word changes the vowel sound (as in **ake** and **ide**). This is the reason for the order in which we introduce the spelling patterns in this book.

Words You Could Make with Simple Patterns in Kindergarten

Here is an *alphabetical list* of some spelling patterns or word families and examples of words that could be made by changing beginning letters. Add the words with **ch**, **sh**, and **th** if you have talked about those letters and the sounds they make together—for example, if you have a Chad, Charlie, Shannon, or Thelma in your room or if you teach those beginning sounds as part of your kindergarten program. If not, these sounds will be taught and talked about as part of *Making Words First Grade*. We have included only words in the vocabulary of most kindergarten students.

ack will help you read and spell **back, Jack, Mack, pack, rack, sack, tack, Zack, black, smack,** and **track** (**shack**)

ad will help you read and spell **bad, dad, had, lad, mad, pad, sad, Tad, glad,** and **Brad** (**Chad**)

ake will help you read and spell **bake, cake, fake, Jake, lake, make, rake, take, wake, Blake, flake,** and **brake** (**shake**)

all will help you read and spell **ball, call, fall, hall, mall, tall, wall, small,** and **stall**

am will help you read and spell **bam, jam, ham, Pam, Sam, yam, clam,** and **slam**

ame will help you read and spell **came, fame, game, name, same, tame, blame,** and **flame** (**shame**)

an will help you read and spell **can, Dan, fan, man, pan, ran, tan, van, plan, scan,** and **Stan** (**than**)

and will help you read and spell **band, hand, land, sand, brand,** and **stand**

ank will help you read and spell **bank, Hank, rank, sank, blank,** and **drank** (**thank**)

ap will help you read and spell **cap, lap, map, nap, rap, sap, clap, slap,** and **snap**

ar will help you read and spell **bar, car, far, jar, tar, scar,** and **star**

at will help you read and spell **bat, cat, fat, hat, mat, pat, Pat, rat, sat, brat, flat,** and **scat** (**chat, that**)

ate will help you read and spell **date, gate, hate, Kate, late, mate, rate, plate,** and **skate**

ay will help you read and spell **day, Fay, hay, Jay, Kay, lay, may, Ray, say, way, clay, play,** and **stay**

eat will help you read and spell **beat, heat, meat, neat, seat, and treat** (**cheat**)

ed will help you read and spell **bed, fed, led, Ned, red, Ted, bled, Fred,** and **sled** (**shed**)

eep will help you read and spell **beep, deep, jeep, keep, weep, steep,** and **sweep** (**sheep**)

ell will help you read and spell **bell, fell, sell, well, yell, smell,** and **spell** (**shell**)

en will help you read and spell **Ben, den, hen, men, pen, ten,** and **Glen** (**then**)

end will help you read and spell **bend, lend, mend, send, blend,** and **spend**

ent will help you read and spell **bent, dent, rent, sent, tent, vent, went, Brent, spent,** and **Trent**

est will help you read and spell **best, pest, rest, test, vest,** and **west** (**chest**)

et will help you read and spell **bet, get, jet, let, met, net, pet, set, vet, wet,** and **yet** (**Chet**)

ick will help you read and spell **Dick, kick, lick, Nick, pick, Rick, sick, tick, stick,** and **trick** (**chick, thick**)

ide will help you read and spell **hide, ride, side, tide, wide, bride, glide,** and **slide**

ill will help you read and spell **Bill, fill, hill, kill, mill, pill, will, still,** and **spill** (**chill**)

in will help you read and spell **bin, fin, kin, pin, sin, tin, win, twin,** and **spin** (**chin, shin, thin**)

ine will help you read and spell **dine, fine, line, mine, nine, pine,** and **vine** (**shine**)

ing will help you read and spell **Bing, ding, king, ring, sing, wing, bring, sting,** and **swing** (**thing**)

ink will help you read and spell **link, mink, pink, rink, sink, wink, blink, drink,** and **stink** (**think**)

ip will help you read and spell **dip, hip, lip, rip, sip, tip, zip, skip, trip,** and **drip** (**chip, ship**)

it will help you read and spell **bit, fit, hit, kit, lit, pit, sit, skit, slit,** and **spit**

ock will help you read and spell **dock, lock, rock, sock, tock, block,** and **clock** (**shock**)

og will help you read and spell **dog, fog, hog, jog, log, frog,** and **smog**

ook will help you read and spell **cook, book, hook, look, took, brook,** and **crook** (**shook**)

op will help you read and spell **bop, hop, mop, pop, top, drop,** and **stop** (**chop, shop**)

ot will help you read and spell **cot, dot, got, hot, lot, not, pot, rot, spot,** and **plot** (**shot**)

ub will help you read and spell **cub, rub, sub, tub, club,** and **stub**

ug will help you read and spell **bug, dug, hug, jug, mug, rug, tug, snug,** and **plug**

ump will help you read and spell **bump, dump, hump, jump, lump, pump, plump,** and **stump** (**thump**)

un will help you read and spell **bun, fun, gun, run,** and **sun**

unk will help you read and spell **bunk, dunk, hunk, junk, sunk, skunk,** and **stunk** (**chunk**)

ut will help you read and spell **but, cut, gut, hut, nut, rut,** and **shut**

The lessons in this book begin with easy, 2-letter patterns. Next, we move to 3-letter patterns where two letters may make the same sound. Finally, we include some lessons with silent letters and vowel sound changes. There are two patterns at the end of the book that are exceptions, **all** and **ook**. Although familiar to young children, they have no easy explanation for their letters and sounds, so we teach these patterns just as a pattern with a sound. Our goal is for all children to practice using letter sounds and learn to blend these letter sounds together to make patterns (or word families or phonograms—the terminology has changed over the years) and then "make words" using these patterns (or word families). When using patterns to make words, we want children to see that changing a letter will make a new word and that many words can be made with each spelling pattern or word family.

Lesson 1
Pattern: at

Letters needed: **a**, t, b, c, f, h, l, m, p, r, and s

1. Books to Read

- *The Cat in the Hat* by Dr. Seuss (Random House, 1957, renewed 1985), ISBN 0-394-80001-X (or read any nonfiction book about cats). Read the book; talk about the title *The Cat in the Hat* and listen for the **at** pattern in **cat** and **hat**. Reread page 6 and have the children listen to the **at** pattern in the words **mat**, **cat**, **hat**, and **that**.

- *Hop on Pop* by Dr. Seuss (Random House, 1963, renewed 1991), ISBN 0-394-80029-X. Read the book; reread pages 26–30, having the children listen for the **at** pattern in **Pat**, **sat**, **hat**, **cat**, **bat**, and **that.**

- *Old Mother Hubbard* illustrated by Jane Babrera (Holiday House, 2001), ISBN 0-8234-1659-3. Read the book; reread pages 8 and 10 and talk about the **at** pattern in **hat** and **cat**.

2. Making Words: Blend letter sounds together to read words

After reading a rhyming book, such as Dr. Seuss's *Cat in the Hat*, and talking about the rhyming words **cat** and **hat**, put the yarned letter cards **a** and **t** on two children, who now represent those two letters. Pass out other yarned letter cards (**b**, **c**, **f**, **h**, **l**, **m**, **p**, **r**, and **s**) to other children in the class. Have the children with the letter cards **a** and **t** stand together. Some teachers ask the **a** and **t** children to hold hands or put their arms around each other. Lead the students to blend these two letter sounds together and say **a/t**, **at**.

Have the letter **c** join **a** and **t** and ask the children to read the word just made. If someone knows the word is **cat** then the teacher and the class blend together the letter sounds **c/a/t** and say **cat**. Use the word **cat** in a sentence: "I once had a big, fat, grey **cat**." Then, have another letter card child (**b**) stand in front of the letters **a** and **t** and ask, "Who can read this word I just made?" Together with the class, blend the three letter sounds to make another word, **b/a/t**, **bat** and use the word in a sentence: "I hit the ball with a **bat**." Continue this way with the letters **f**, **h**, **m**, **p**, **r**, and **s** (**f/a/t**, **fat**; **h/a/t**, **hat**; **m/a/t**, **mat**; **p/a/t**, **pat**, **Pat**; **r/a/t**, **rat**; and **s/a/t**, **sat**). Since a name can be made with this pattern, talk about names and how when making the name **Pat** they need to turn their letter cards around to the capital letter side. Say, "Names, just like your name, need a capital letter at the beginning." End the lesson by blending two letters together. This is more difficult for kindergartners and makes the lesson more multilevel.

3. Making Words: Blend and segment to spell words

Do another round of Making Words with the letter cards, this time not only blending and segmenting (taking away) sounds but also listening for what letter the children need to spell a word. Stand in front of the class or group and have the letters **a** and **t** stand together once again; ask the two **a** and **t** children to hold hands or put their arms around each other. Blend these two letter sounds and lead the class to say **at**. Using the **at** pattern, say, "**Cat**—Point to the letter we need to come and stand in front of **at** to make the word **cat**." See that **c** comes and stands with **at**, lead the class to say **c/at**, **cat**. The letter **c** leaves (segmenting) and **at** is left standing alone. Then use the **at** pattern to do a second round of Making Words, asking, What letter do we need to make (spell) **hat**? **bat**? **fat**? **mat**? **pat**? **Pat**? **rat**? **sat**? **brat**? **flat**? (**chat**? **that**?). The children wearing the needed letters will join the two children with **at**—holding their yarned letter cards (**h, b, f, m, p, P, r, s**) in front of **at** to spell or make the words. If a name can be made with the pattern, then talk about names and capital letters and see that the child turns around the letter card to the capital side.

4. Collect the Letter Cards

Call for each letter to review the letter names. When the children have made words with the **at** pattern and have read and spelled the words, collect the letter cards by saying, "Will the person who has the **a** bring it to me. Will the person with the letter **t** bring it to me," continuing in any order until all the letter cards are collected. This final activity will help those students who still need practice with letter names.

Lesson 2
Pattern: am

Letters needed: **a**, **m**, **b**, **h**, **j**, **l**, **p**, **r**, **s**, and **y**

1. Books to Read

- *Green Eggs and Ham and Sam I Am* by Dr. Seuss (Random House, 1960, renewed 1988), ISBN 13: 978-0-375-84165-1. Read the book; reread the first 12 pages and talk about the **am** pattern in **am**, **Sam**, and **ham**.

- *Miss Spider's New Car* written and illustrated by David Kirk (Scholastic, 1997), ISBN 0-590-30713-4. Read the book; then reread the page with the **am** pattern and talk about the **am** pattern in **ma'am** and **am**.

- *Hello School* by Dee Lillegard (Dragonfly Books, 2003), ISBN 0-44041-777-5. Read the book; reread the page with **bam** and **am** and talk about the **am** pattern.

2. Making Words: Blend and segment to read words

First, make the pattern **am** with the letter card children. Lead the children to say the letter sounds and pattern **a/m**, **am**. Then, using the letter card **j**, ask, "Who can read this word?" Together with the class, blend the letter sounds and say **j/a/m**, **jam**. Use the word in a sentence: "I like strawberry **jam**!" Continue this way with the other letters to make and read **b/a/m**, **bam**; **h/a/m**, **ham**; **P/a/m**, **Pam**; **S/a/m**, **Sam**; and **y/a/m**, **yam.** Remember to use the capital letter side for the names **Pam** and **Sam**. Using two letters together, make and read the words **cl/am**, **clam** and **sl/am**, **slam**.

3. Making Words: Blend and segment to spell words

After making and reading words, use the same letter cards and lead the class to spell some words. Ask the class to point to the letter to put in front of **am** to make (spell) the word **jam**. Continue the same way with **bam**, **ham**, **Pam**, **ram**, **Sam**, **yam**, **clam**, and **slam**.

4. Collect the Letter Cards

Call for each letter to review the letter names.

Lesson 3
Pattern: ad

Letters needed: a, d (2), b, g, h, l, m, p, s, and r

1. Books to Read

- *Hop on Pop* by Dr. Seuss (Random House, 1963, renewed 1991), ISBN 0-394-80029-X. Read pages 32–33 and talk about the **ad** pattern in the words **sad**, **dad**, **bad**, and **had.**

- *I Can Read with My Eyes Shut!* by Dr. Seuss (Random House, 1978), ISBN 0-394-83912-9. Read the book; reread pages 22 and 23 and talk about the **ad** pattern in **sad**, **glad**, and **mad.**

- *One Fish, Two Fish, Red Fish, Blue Fish* by Dr. Seuss (Random House, 1960, renewed 1988), ISBN 10: 0-375-84166-0. Read the book; reread pages 5 and 6 and talk about the **ad** pattern in **sad**, **glad**, **bad**, and **dad.**

2. Making Words: Blend and segment to read words

First, make the pattern **ad** with the letter card children. Lead the children to say the letter sounds and pattern **a/d**, **ad**. Then make and read a word using one of the other letter cards (**b**) and ask, "Who can read this word?" Together with the class, blend the letter sounds and say **b/a/d**, **bad**. Use the word in a sentence: "Yesterday was a **bad** day." Continue this way with the other letters to make and read **d/a/d**, **dad**; **h/a/d**, **had**; **l/a/d**, **lad**; **m/a/d**, **mad**; **p/a/d**, **pad**; **s/a/d**, **sad**; and **T/ad**, **Tad**. Use two letter sounds together at the beginning of the word to make and read **Brad** and **glad**. (If you have taught your class the **ch** sound, add **Chad**.)

3. Making Words: Blend and segment to spell words

After making and reading words, use the same letter cards and lead the class to spell some words. Ask the class to point to the letter to put in front of **ad** to make the word **bad**. Continue to make and spell **dad**, **had**, **lad mad**, **pad**, **sad**, **Brad**, and **glad** (**Chad**). Remember capital letters for names.

4. Collect the Letter Cards

Call for each letter to review the letter names.

Lesson 4
Pattern: ap

Letters needed: **a**, **p**, **c**, **l**, **m**, **n**, **r**, and **s**

1. Books to Read

- *The Three Billy Goats Gruff* retold by Annette Smith (Rigby, in the PM Traditional Tales and Plays Collection, 1997), ISBN 0-7635-1971-5 (or any of the books about the Three Billy Goats). Read the book; then reread page 6, 10, or 14 and talk about the **ap** pattern in "Trip-**trap**, trip-**trap**, trip-**trap**."
- *Sheep in a Ship* by Nancy Shaw (Houghton Mifflin, 1986), ISBN 395-48160-0. Read the book; reread page 10 and talk about the **ap** pattern in **lap**, **flap**, and **nap**.

2. Making Words: Blend and segment to read words

First, make the pattern **ap** with the letter card children. Lead the children to say the letter sounds and pattern **a/p**, **ap**. Then make and read a word using one of the other letter cards (**n**) and ask, "Who can read this word?" Together with the class, blend the letter sounds and say **n/a/p**, **nap**. Use the word in a sentence: "The little boy took a **nap**." Continue this way with the other letters to make and read **c/a/p**, **cap**; **l/a/p**, **lap**; **m/a/p**, **map**; **r/a/p**, **rap**; and **s/a/p/**, **sap**. Use two letter sounds together at the beginning of the word to make and read **clap**, **slap**, and **snap**.

3. Making Words: Blend and segment to spell words

After making and reading words, use the same letter cards and lead the class to spell some words. Ask the class to point to the letter to put in front of **a-p** to make the word **nap**. Continue to make and spell **cap**, **lap**, **map**, **nap**, **rap**, **sap**, **clap**, **slap**, and **snap**.

4. Collect the Letter Cards

Call for each letter to review the letter names.

Lesson 5
Pattern: an

Letters needed: a, n, c, d, f, m, l, p, r, s, t, and v

1. Books to Read

- *The Gingerbread Man*, retold by Alan Trussel-Cullen (Dominie Press, 1999), ISBN 0-7685-0412-0 (or any Gingerbread Man book). Read the book; reread page 5 and talk about the **an** pattern in the Gingerbread **Man**, **ran**, and **woman**.

- *I Can Read with My Eyes Shut!* by Dr. Seuss (Random House, 1978), ISBN 0-394-83912-9. Read the book; then reread the first few pages and talk about the **an** pattern in **can**.

- *Pat-a-Cake, Pat-a-Cake*, found in any book of nursery rhymes. Read the rhyme and talk about the **an** pattern in **man** and **can**.

2. Making Words: Blend and segment to read words

First, make the pattern **an** with the letter card children. Lead the children to say the letter sounds and pattern **a/n**, **an**. Then make and read a word using one of the other letter cards (**c**) and ask, "Who can read this word?" Together with the class, blend the letter sounds and say **c/a/n**, **can**. Then use the word in a sentence: "I **can** do it!" Continue this way with the other letters to make and read **D/a/n**, **Dan**; **f/a/n**, **fan**; **m/a/n**, **man**; **p/a/n**, **pan**; **r/a/n**, **ran**; **t/a/n**, **tan**; and **v/a/n**, **van**. Use two letter sounds together at the beginning of the word to make and read **plan**, **scan**, and **Stan** (If you have taught **th**, add **than**.) Remember the capital letter for names.

3. Making Words: Blend and segment to spell words

After making and reading words, use the same letter cards and lead the class to spell some words. Ask the class to point to the letter to put in front of **a-n** to make the word **can**. Continue to make and spell **Dan**, **fan**, **man**, **pan**, **ran**, **tan**, **van**, **plan**, **scan**, and **Stan** (**than**).

4. Collect the Letter Cards

Call for each letter to review the letter names.

Lesson 6

Review Patterns:
at, am, ad, ap, and an

Letter cards needed for this review lesson: **a, t, c, d, h, m, n,** and **p**

Words to make (read and spell) together:

1. cat
2. mat
3. man
4. pan
5. nap
6. cap
7. Pam
8. ham
9. mad
10. pad

For this review lesson have the children give you a sentence for each word they make.

After the lesson read or reread a book with one or more of these patterns in it for transfer.

Lesson 7
Pattern: ed

Letters needed: e, d, b, f, l, n, s, r, and t

1. Books to Read

- *Fred and Ted Go Camping* by Peter Eastman (Random House, 2005), ISBN 0-375-82965-2. Read the book; talk about the names **Fred** and **Ted** and have the children listen to the **ed** pattern in **Fred** and **Ted** and talk about this pattern.

- *Mouse Mess* by Linnea Riley (Scholastic, 1997), IBSN 0-590-10050-5. Read the book; reread the last three pages and talk about the **ed** pattern and sound in **fed** and **bed**.

- *Hop on Pop* by Dr. Seuss (Random House 1963, renewed 1991), ISBN 0-394-80029-X. Read the book; reread pages 22–25 and listen for the **ed** pattern in **red**, **bed**, **Ned**, **Ted**, and **Ed**.

2. Making Words: Blend and segment to read words

First, make the pattern **ed** with the letter card children. Lead the children to say the letter sounds and pattern **e/d, ed**. Then make and read a word using one of the other letter cards (**b**) and ask, "Who can read this word?" Together with the class, blend the letter sounds and say **b/e/d, bed**. Use the word in a sentence: "At night I sleep in my **bed**." Continue this way with the other letters to make and read **f/e/d, fed**; **l/e/d, led**; **N/e/d, Ned**; **r/e/d, red**; and **T/e/d, Ted**. Use two letter sounds together at the beginning of the word to make and read **bled, sled, Fred** (and **shed** if you have already taught the **sh** sound.). Remember to talk about and use the capital letters for names **Ned, Ted**, and **Fred**.

3. Making Words: Blend and segment to spell words

Use the same letter cards and lead the class to spell words. Ask the class to point to the letter to put in front of **e-d** to make the word **bed**. Continue to spell **fed, led, Ned, red, Ted, bled, sled**, and **Fred** (**shed**).

4. Collect the Letter Cards

Call for each letter to review the letter names.

Lesson 8
Pattern: et

Letters needed: e, t, b, g, j, l, m, n, p, s, v, w, and y

1. Books to Read

- *Hunky Dory Ate It* by Katie Evans (Puffin Unicorn Books, 1992), ISBN 0-14-055856-X (or read any nonfiction book about pets). Read the book; reread page 12 of text in the book and talk about the **et** pattern in **pet** and **vet**.

- *One Fish, Two Fish, Red Fish, Blue Fish* by Dr. Seuss (Random House, 1960, renewed 1988), ISBN 10: 0-375-84166-0. Read the book; reread page 48 and talk about the **et** pattern in **pet**, **wet**, **yet**, **bet**, and **get.**

- *Hop on Pop* by Dr. Seuss (Random House 1963, renewed 1991), ISBN 0-394-80029-X. Read the book; reread page 54 and listen for the **et** pattern in **wet** and **get.**

2. Making Words: Blend and segment to read words

First, make the pattern **et** with the letter card children. Lead the children to say the letter sounds and pattern **e-t/et**. Then make and read a word using one of the other letter cards (**p**) and ask, "Who can read this word?" Together with the class, blend the letter sounds and say **p/e/t, pet**. Use the word in a sentence: "Do you have a **pet**?" Continue this way with the other letters to make and read **b/e/t, bet**; **g/e/t, get**; **j/e/t, jet**; **l/e/t, let**; **m/e/t, met**; **n/e/t, net**; **s/e/t, set**; **v/e/t, vet**; **w/e/t, wet**; and **y/e/t, yet** (If you have taught the **ch** sound, add **Chet**.) Talk about names and capital letters.

3. Making Words: Blend and segment to spell words

After making and reading words, use the same letter cards and lead the class to spell words. Ask the class to point to the letter to put in front of **e-t** to make the word **pet**. Continue to make and spell **bet**, **get**, **jet**, **let**, **met**, **net**, **set**, **vet**, **wet**, and **yet** (**Chet**).

4. Collect the Letter Cards

Call for each letter to review the letter names.

Lesson 9
Pattern: en

Letters needed: e, n, b, d, g, h, l, m, p, and t

1. Books to Read

- *The Little Red Hen* retold by Alan Trussell-Cullen (Dominie Press, 1999), ISBN 0-7685-0408-2. Read the book; talk about the title and the name *Little Red **Hen***.

- *Who's in the Shed?* by Brenda Parkes (Rigby, 1986), ISBN 0-7312-0028-4. Read the book; reread page 10 and talk about the **en** pattern in **then** and **hen**.

- *If the Shoe Fits* by Allison Jackson (Holt, 2001), ISBN 0-80506-466-4. Read the book; reread the page with the words **men** and **then** and talk about this **en** pattern.

2. Making Words: Blend and segment to read words

First, make the pattern **en** with the letter card children. Lead the children to say the letter sounds and pattern **e-n/en**. Then make and read a word using one of the other letter cards (**t**) and ask, "Who can read this word?" Together with the class, blend the letter sounds and say **t-e-n/ten**. Use the word in a sentence: "I can count to **ten**." Continue this way with the other letters to make and read **B/e/n**, **Ben**; **d/e/n**, **den**; **h/e/n**, **hen**; **m/e/n**, **men**; and **p/e/n**, **pen**. Use two letter sounds toether at the beginning of the word to make and read **Glen**. (If you have taught the **th** sound, add **then**.) Remember the capital letter for names.

3. Making Words: Blend and segment to spell words

After making and reading words, use the same letter cards and lead the class to spell words. Ask the class to point to the letter to put in front of **e-n** to make the word **ten**. Continue to make and spell **Ben**, **den**, **hen**, **men**, **pen**, **ten**, and **Glen** (**then**).

4. Collect the Letter Cards

Call for each letter to review the letter names.

Lesson 10
Pattern: ell

Letters needed: e, l (2), **b, f, m, p, s, w,** and **y**

1. Books to Read

- *The Brand New Kid* by Katie Couric (Doubleday, 2000), ISBN 0-385-50030-0. Read the book; reread page 4 and talk about the **ell** pattern in **well** and **swell**.
- *Tumble Bumble* by Felicia Bond (Scholastic, 1996), ISBN 0-590-12710-1. Read the book; reread page 14 and talk about the **ell** pattern in **bell** and **well**.
- *The Night Before Summer Vacation* by Natasha Wing (Grosset and Dunlap, 2002), ISBN 0-448-42830-X. Read the book; reread page 13 and talk about the **ell** pattern in **shell** and **swell** (or you can read a nonfiction book about shells).

2. Making Words: Blend and segment to read words

First, make the pattern **ell** with the letter card children. *Explain that the two l's together make one l sound.* Lead the children to say the letter sound and pattern, **e/ll, ell.** Then make and read a word using one of the other letter cards (**b**) and ask, "Who can read this word?" Together with the class, blend the letter sounds and say **b/e/ll, bell.** Use the word in a sentence: "I hear the **bell**." Continue this way with the other letters to make and read **f/e/ll, fell; s/e/ll, sell; w/e/ll, well;** and **y/e/ll, yell.** Use two letter sounds together at the beginning of the word to make and read **smell** and **spell.** (If you have taught the **sh** sound, add **shell.**)

3. Making Words: Blend and segment to spell words

After making and reading words, use the same letter cards and lead the class to spell some words. Ask the class to point to the letter to put in front of **ell** to make the word **bell.** Continue to make and spell **fell, sell, well, yell, smell,** and **spell** (**shell**).

4. Collect the Letter Cards

Call for each letter to review the letter names.

Lesson 11
Pattern: est

Letters needed: e, s, t, b, p, r, t (2), w, and v

1. Books to Read

- *I Ain't Gonna Paint No More!* by Karen Beaumont (Harcourt, 2005), ISBN 0-15-202488-3. Read the book; reread pages 15–17 and talk about the **est** pattern in **rest** and **chest**.

- *Today I Feel Silly and Other Moods that Make My Day* by Jamie Lee Curtis (Joanna Cotler [HarperCollins Imprint], 1998), ISBN 0-06-024560-3. Read the book; reread page 20 and talk about the **est** pattern in **best** and **test**.

- *How I Spent My Summer Vacation* by Mark Teague (Dragonfly Books, 1995), ISBN 0-517-517-59999-8. Read the book; reread the first page and talk about the **est** pattern in **west** and **rest**.

2. Making Words: Blend and segment to read words

First, make the pattern **est** with the letter card children and explain that three letters make this **est** pattern. Lead the children to blend these three letters together and say **e/s/t**, **est**. Then make and read a word using one of the other letter cards (**p**) and ask, "Who can read this word?" Together with the class, blend the letter sounds and say **p/e/s/t**, **pest**. Use the word in a sentence: "My sister is a **pest**." Continue this way with the other letters to make and read **b/e/s/t**, **best**; **r/e/s/t**, **rest**; **t/e/s/t**, **test**; **w/e/s/t**, **west**; and **v/e/s/t**, **vest**. (If your students know the sound of **ch**, then have them make and read **chest**.)

3. Making Words: Blend and segment to spell words

After making and reading words, use the same letter cards and lead the class to spell words. Ask the class to point to the letter to put in front of **est** to make the word **pest**. Continue to make and spell **best**, **rest**, **test**, **west**, and **vest** (**chest**).

4. Collect the Letter Cards

Call for each letter to review the letter names.

Review Patterns:
ed, et, en, ell, and est

Letter cards needed for this review lesson: e, b, d, l (2), n, r, s, and t

Words to make (read and spell) together:

1. net
2. set
3. sell
4. bell
5. Ben
6. ten
7. Ted
8. bed
9. best
10. rest

For this review lesson have the children give you a sentence for each word they make.

After the lesson read or reread a book with one or more of these patterns in it for transfer.

Lesson 13
Pattern: it

Letters needed: **i**, **t**, **b**, **f**, **h**, **k**, **l**, **p**, and **s**

1. Books to Read

- *The Cat in the Hat* by Dr. Seuss (Random House, 1957, renewed 1985), ISBN 0-394-80001-X. Read the book; reread page 3 and talk about the **it** pattern in the words **sit**, **it**, and **bit**.

- *How I Spent My Summer Vacation* by Mark Teague (Dragonfly Books, 1995), ISBN 0-517-517-59999-8. Read the book; reread page 11 and talk about the **it** pattern in **sit** and **quit**.

- *Inchworm and a Half* by Elinor T. Pinczer (Houghton Mifflin, 2003), ISBN 0-61831-101-7. Read the book; reread page 8 and talk about the **it** pattern in **bit** and **fit**.

2. Making Words: Blend and segment to read words

First, make the pattern **it** with the letter card children. Lead the children to say the letter sounds and pattern **i/t**, **it**. Then make and read a word using one of the other letter cards (**f**) and ask, "Who can read this word?" Together with the class, blend the letter sounds and say **f/i/t**, **fit**. Use the word in a sentence: "My new shoes **fit**." Continue this way with the other letters to make and read **b/i/t**, **bit**; **h/i/t**, **hit**; **k/i/t**, **kit**; **l/i/t**, **lit**; **p/i/t**, **pit**; and **s/i/t**, **sit**. Use two letter sounds together at the beginning of the word make and read **skit**, **slit**, and **spit**.

3. Making Words: Blend and segment to spell words

After making and reading words, use the same letter cards and lead the class to spell words. Ask the class to point to the letter to put in front of **i-t** to make the word **fit**. Continue to make and spell **bit**, **fit**, **hit**, **lit**, **pit**, **sit**, **skit**, **slit**, and **spit**.

4. Collect the Letter Cards

Call for each letter to review the letter names.

Lesson 14
Pattern: in

Letters needed: **i, n, b, f, k, p, s, t,** and **w**

1. Books to Read

- *The Three Little Pigs*, retold by Alan Trussell-Cullen (Dominie Press, 1999), ISBN 0-76850410-4. Read the book; reread page 7, 9, or 11 and talk about the **in** pattern in **chinny-chin chin** and **in**.

- *Here Are My Hands* by Bill Martin Jr. and John Archambault (Henry Holt, 1989), ISBN 0-8050-1168-4. Read the book; reread the last two pages and talk about the **in** pattern in **chin**, **skin**, and **in**.

- *Counting Is for the Birds* by Frank Mazzola Jr. (Charlesbridge, 1997), ISBN 0-88106-950-7. Read the book; reread the page with **in** and **spin** and talk about the **in** pattern.

2. Making Words: Blend and segment to read words

First, make the pattern **in** with the letter card children. Lead the children to say the letter sounds and pattern **i/n**, **in**. Then make and read a word using one of the other letter cards (**w**) and ask, "Who can read this word?" Together with the class, blend the letter sounds and say **w/i/n**, **win**. Use the word in a sentence: "I hope we **win** the ball game." Continue this way with the other letters to make and read **b/i/n, bin; f/i/n, fin; k/i/n, kin; p/i/n, pin; s/i/n, sin;** and **t/i/n, tin**. Use two letter sounds together at the beginning of the word to make and read the words **twin** and **spin** (**chin**, **thin**, and **shin**).

3. Making Words: Blend and segment to spell words

After making and reading words, use the same letter cards and lead the class to spell words. Ask the class to point to the letter to put in front of **i-n** to make the word **win**. Continue to make and spell **bin**, **fin**, **kin**, **pin**, **tin**, **twin**, and **spin** (**chin**, **thin**, and **shin**).

4. Collect the Letter Cards

Call for each letter to review the letter names.

Lesson 15
Pattern: ip

Letters needed: **i**, **p**, **d**, **h**, **k**, **l**, **r**, **s**, **t**, and **z**

1. Books to Read

- *Miss Bindergarten Stays Home from Kindergarten* by Joseph Slate (Dutton Children's Books, 2000), ISBN 0-525-46396-8. Read the book; reread pages 19 and 20 and talk about the **ip** pattern in **sip** and **dip**.

- *Animal A B Cs* by Susan Hood (Troll, 1995), ISBN 0-8167-3572-7. Read this ABC book; reread the Ii page and talk about the **ip** pattern in **grip** and **slip**.

- *If the Shoe Fits* by Alison Jackson (Henry Holt, 2001), ISBN 0-80506-466-1. Read the book; reread the page with the **ip** patterns and talk about the **ip** in **sip** and **lip**.

2. Making Words: Blend and segment to read words

First, make the pattern **ip** with the letter card children. Lead the children to say the letter sounds and pattern **i-p/ip**. Then make and read a word using one of the other letter cards (**l**) and ask, "Who can read this word?" Together with the class, blend the letter sounds and say **l/i/p**, **lip**. Use the word in a sentence: "I bit my **lip**." Continue this way with the other letters to make and read **d/i/p**, **dip**; **h/i/p**, **hip**; **r/i/p**, **rip**; **s/i/p**, **sip**; **t/i/p**, **tip**; and **z/i/p**, **zip**. Use two letter sounds together at the beginning of the word to make and read **drip**, **skip**, and **trip** (**chip** and **ship**).

3. Making Words: Blend and segment to spell words

After making and reading words, use the same letter cards and lead the class to spell words. Ask the class to point to the letter to put in front of **i-p** to make the word **lip**. Continue to make and spell **dip**, **hip**, **rip**, **sip**, **tip**, **zip**, **drip**, **skip**, and **trip** (**chip** and **ship**).

4. Collect the Letter Cards

Call for each letter to review the letter names.

Lesson 16
Pattern: ill

Letters needed: i, l (2), b, f, h, k, m, p, s, t, and w

1. Books to Read

- *Each Peach Pear Plum* by Janet and Allen Ahlberg (Viking Press and Scholastic, 1978), ISBN 0-590-41081-4. Read the book; reread page 14, "Bo-Peep up the **hill.** I spy Jack and **Jill.** Talk about the **ill** pattern.

- *Counting Is for the Birds* by Frank Mazzola (Charlesbridge Publishing, 1997), ISBN 0-88106-950-7. Read the book; reread the page with the **ill** pattern and talk about the **ill** pattern in **fill** and **skill.**

- *Hop on Pop* by Dr. Seuss (Random House, 1963, renewed 1991), ISBN 0-394-80029-X. Read the book; reread pages 56 and 57 and listen for the **ill** pattern in **hill, Will,** and **still.**

2. Making Words: Blend and segment to read words

First, make the pattern **ill** with the letter card children. Tell the children that the two **l**'s make one **l** sound. Lead the children to say the letter sounds and pattern **i/ll, ill.** Then make and read a word using one of the other letter cards (**h**) and ask, "Who can read this word?" Together with the class, blend the letter sounds and say **h/i/ll, hill.** Use the word in a sentence: "Up the **hill** we go." Continue this way with the other letters to make and read **B/i/ll, Bill; f/i/ll, fill: h/i/ll, hill; k/i/ll, kill; m/i/ll, mill; p/i/ll, pill;** and **w/i/ll, will.** Remember to talk about the capital letter for **Bill.** Use two letter sounds together with the pattern to make and read **still** and **spill** (**chill**).

3. Making Words: Blend and segment to spell words

After making and reading words, use the same letter cards and lead the class to spell words. Ask the class to point to the letter to put in front of **ill** to make the word **hill.** Continue to make and spell **Bill, hill, kill, mill, pill, will, still,** and **spill** (**chill**).

4. Collect the Letter Cards

Call for each letter to review the letter names.

Lesson 17
Pattern: ick

Letters needed: i, c, k (2), d, l, n, p, r, s, and t

1. Books to Read

- *Miss Bindergarten Stays Home from Kindergarten* by Joseph Slate (Dutton Children's Books, 2000), ISBN 0-525-46396-8. Read the book; reread pages 21 and 22 and talk about the **ick** pattern in **trick** and **sick**.

- *Animal A B Cs* by Susan Hood (Troll, 1995), ISBN 0-8167-3572-7. Read this ABC book; reread page C and talk about the **ick** pattern in **trick** and **lick**.

- *Jack Be Nimble* found in any collection of nursery rhymes. Read the rhyme and talk about the **ick** pattern in **quick** and **stick**.

2. Making Words: Blend and segment to read words

First, make the pattern **ick** with the letter card children. Tell the children that the **c** and **k** make one sound. Lead the children to say the letter sounds and pattern **i/ck**, **ick**. Then make and read a word using one of the other letter cards (**p**) and ask, "Who can read this word?" Together with the class, blend the letter sounds and say **p/i/ck**, /**pick**. Use the word in a sentence: "I like to **pick** blackberries." Continue this way with the other letters to make and read **D/i/ck**, **Dick**; **k/i/ck**, **kick**; **l/i/ck**, **lick**; **N/i/ck**, **Nick**, **s/i/ck**, **sick**; **t/i/ck**, **tick**; and **R/i/ck**, **Rick**. Remember to use and talk about capital letters for the names **Dick**, **Nick**, and **Rick**. Use two letter sounds together with the pattern to make and read the words **stick** and **trick** (**chick** and **thick**).

3. Making Words: Blend and segment to spell words

After making and reading words, use the same letter cards and lead the class to spell words. Ask the class to point to the letter to put in front of **ick** to make the word **pick**. Continue to make and spell **Dick**, **kick**, **lick**, **Nick**, **sick**, **tick**, **Rick**, **stick**, and **trick** (**chick** and **thick**).

4. Collect the Letter Cards

Call for each letter to review the letter names.

Lesson 18

Review Patterns:
it, in, ip, ill, and ick

Letter cards needed for this review lesson: i, b, c, k, l (2), n, p, s, t, and w

Words to make (read and spell) together:

1. win
2. pin
3. sip
4. lip
5. pill
6. Bill
7. bit
8. sit
9. sick
10. lick

For this review lesson have the children give you a sentence for each word they make.

After the lesson read or reread a book with one or more of these patterns in it for transfer.

Lesson 19
Pattern: op

Letters needed: **o, p** (2), **b, d, h, m, t, s,** and **r**

1. Books to Read

- *Hop on Pop* by Dr. Seuss (Random House, 1963, renewed 1991), ISBN 0-394-80029-X. Read the book; reread the pages 40 and 41 and listen for the **op** pattern in **hop, pop,** and **stop.**

- *Ten Apples Up on Top* by Theo LeSieg (Random House, 1961), ISBN 0-394-80019-2. Read the book; reread pages 19 through 21 and talk about the **op** pattern in the words **stop, top,** and **drop.**

- *One Fish, Two Fish, Red Fish, Blue Fish* by Dr. Seuss (Random House, 1960, renewed 1988), ISBN 10: 0-375-84166-0. Read the book; reread pages 44 and 45 and talk about the **op** pattern in **hop, Yop, top,** and **Pop.**

2. Making Words: Blend and segment to read words

First, make the pattern **op** with the letter card children. Lead the children to say the letter sounds and pattern **o/p, op.** Then make and read a word using one of the other letter cards (**h**) and ask, "Who can read this word?" Together with the class, blend the letter sounds and say **h/o/p, hop.** Use the word in a sentence: "See the rabbit **hop.**" Continue this way with the other letters to make and read **b/o/p, bop; m/o/p, mop; p/o/p, pop;** and **t/o/p, top.** Use two letter sounds together with the pattern to make and read the words **stop,** and **drop.** (If you have taught the **ch** and **sh** sounds, make and read the words **chop** and **shop.**)

3. Making Words: Blend and segment to spell words

After making and reading words, use the same letter cards and lead the class to spell words. Ask the class to point to the letter to put in front of **op** to make the word **hop.** Continue to make and spell **bop, mop, pop, top, stop,** and **drop** (**chop** and **shop**).

4. Collect the Letter Cards

Call for each letter to review the letter names.

Lesson 20
Pattern: ot

Letters needed: o, t, c, d, h, g, l, p, and s

1. Books to Read

- *The Cat in the Hat* by Dr. Seuss (Random House, 1957, renewed 1985), ISBN 0-394-80001-X. Read the book; reread page 27 and point out the **ot** pattern in **lot** and **pot**; page 35 (**not** and **pot**); and page 39 (**not** and **pot**).

- *I Can Read with My Eyes Shut!* by Dr. Seuss (Random House, 1978), ISBN 0-394-83912-9. Read the book; reread page 8 and talk about the **ot** pattern in **hot** and **lot**.

2. Making Words: Blend and segment to read words

First, make the pattern **ot** with the letter card children. Lead the children to say the letter sounds and pattern **o/t**, **ot**. Then make and read a word using one of the other letter cards (**p**) and ask, "Who can read this word?" Together with the class, blend the letter sounds and say **p/o/t**, **pot**. Use the word in a sentence: "I cook my soup in a **pot**." Continue this way with the other letters to make and read **c/o/t**, **cot**; **d/o/t**, **dot**; **h/o/t**, **hot**; **g/o/t**, **got**; **l/o/t**, **lot**; **n/o/t**, **not**; and **r/o/t**, **rot**. Use two letter sounds together with the pattern to make and read **spot** and **plot** (**shot**).

3. Making Words: Blend and segment to spell words

After making and reading words, use the same letter cards and lead the class to spell words. Ask the class to point to the letter to put in front of **ot** to make the word **pot**. Continue to make and spell **cot**, **dot**, **hot**, **got**, **lot**, **not**, **rot**, **spot**, and **plot** (**shot**).

4. Collect the Letter Cards

Call for each letter to review the letter names.

Lesson 21
Pattern: og

Letters needed: o, g, d, f, h, l, m, r, and s

1. Books to Read

- *The Flea's Sneeze* by Lynn Downey (Holt, 2000), ISBN 0-80506-103-7. Read the book and listen for the **og** in **hog** and **frog** on page 3 and **frog**, **log**, and **hog** on page 7.

- *The Grumpy Morning* by Pamela Duncan Edwards (Hyperion Books, 1998), ISBN 0786803312, 978-0786803316. Read the book; reread the page with the **og** pattern and talk about it in **dog** and **hog**.

- *Miss Spider's New Car* by David Kirk (Scholastic, 1997), ISBN 0-590-30713-4. Read the book; reread page 1 and talk about the **og** pattern in **frog** and **bog**.

- *To Market, To Market,* found in any collection of nursery rhymes. Read the rhyme and talk about the **og** pattern in **hog** and **jog**.

2. Making Words: Blend and segment to read words

First, make the pattern **og** with the letter card children. Lead the children to say the letter sounds and pattern **o/g**, **og**. Then make and read a word using one of the other letter cards (**d**) and ask, "Who can read this word?" Together with the class, blend the letter sounds and say **d/o/g**, **dog**. Use the word in a sentence: "My **dog** likes to play." Continue this way with the other letters to make and read **f/o/g**, **fog**; **h/o/g**, **hog**; **j/o/g**, **jog**; and **l/o/g**, **log**. Use two letter sounds together with the pattern to make and read the words **frog** and **smog.**

3. Making Words: Blend and segment to spell words

After making and reading words, use the same letter cards and lead the class to spell words. Ask the class to point to the letter to put in front of **og** to make the word **dog**. Continue to make and spell **fog**, **hog**, **jog**, **log**, **frog**, and **smog**.

4. Collect the Letter Cards

Call for each letter to review the letter names.

Lesson 22
Pattern: ock

Letters needed: **o, c** (2), **k, b, d, l, r,** and **s**

1. Books to Read

- *Boy, You're Amazing!* by Virginia Kroll (Albert Whitman, 2004), ISBN 0-8075-0868-3. Read the book; reread pages 3 and 4 and talk about the **ock** pattern in **clock** and **block.**

- *If the Shoe Fits* by Allison Jackson (Holt, 2001), ISBN 0-80506-466-4. Read the book; reread the page with the **ock** pattern and let the children listen to the **ock** pattern in **sock** and **clock.**

- *Hickory Dickory Dock*, found in any collection of nursery rhymes. Read the rhyme and talk about the **ock** pattern in **dock** and **clock.**

2. Making Words: Blend and segment to read words

First, make the pattern **ock** with the letter card children. Tell the children that the **c** and **k** make one sound. Lead the children to say the letter sounds and pattern **o/ck, ock.** Then make and read a word using one of the other letter cards (**r**) and ask, "Who can read this word?" Together with the class, blend the letter sounds and say **r/o/ck, rock.** Use the word in a sentence: "See the pretty, white **rock.**" Continue this way with the other letters to make and read **d/o/ck, dock; l/o/ck, lock; s/o/ck, sock;** and **t/o/ck, tock.** Use two letter sounds together with the pattern to read and spell the words **block** and **clock** (**shock**).

3. Making Words: Blend and segment to spell words

After making and reading words, use the same letter cards and lead the class to spell words. Ask the class to point to the letter to put in front of **ock** to make the word **rock.** Continue to make and spell **dock, lock, sock, tock, block,** and **clock** (**shock**).

4. Collect the Letter Cards

Call for each letter to review the letter names.

Lesson 23

Review Patterns:
op, ot, og, and ock

Letter cards needed for this review lesson: **o, c, d, f, g, h, k, p, s,** and **t**

Words to make (read and spell) together:

1. dog
2. fog
3. got
4. hot
5. hog
6. log
7. lock
8. sock
9. stop
10. hop

For this review lesson have the children give you a sentence for each word they make.

After the lesson read or reread a book with one or more of these patterns in it for transfer.

Lesson 24
Pattern: ug

Letters needed: **u**, **g**, **b**, **d**, **h**, **j**, **l**, **m**, **n**, **p**, **r**, **s**, and **t**

1. Books to Read

- *Sheep in a Shop* by Nancy Shaw (Houghton Mifflin, 1991, renewed 1996), ISBN 0-395-73329-4. Read the book; reread page 19 and talk about the **ug** pattern in **tug** and **shrug**.

- *There's a Bug in My Mug*! by Kent Salisbury (McClanahan, 1997), ISBN 1-56293-931-9. Read the book; talk about the **ug** pattern in the title and in the first set of rhymes: Who's in my **mug**? A big green **bug**!

- *Lunch Money and Other Poems About School* by Carol Diggory Shields (Puffin Penguin Books, 1995), ISBN 0-525-45345-8. Read the poem on page 31 and talk about the **ug** pattern in **bug** and **shug**.

2. Making Words: Blend and segment to read words

First, make the pattern **ug** with the letter card children. Lead the children to say the letter sounds and pattern **u/g**, **ug**. Then make and read a word using one of the other letter cards (**b**) and ask, "Who can read this word?" Together with the class, blend the letter sounds and say **b/u/g**, **bug**. Use the word in a sentence: "See the little **bug**." Continue this way with the other letters to make and read **d/u/g**, **dug**; **h/u/g**, **hug**; **j/u/g**, **jug**; **m/u/g**, **mug**; **r/u/g**, **rug**; and **t/u/g**, **tug**. Use two letter sounds together with the pattern to make and read **snug** and **plug**.

3. Making Words: Blend and segment to spell words

Lead the class to spell words by asking the children to point to the letter to put in front of **ug** to make the word **bug**. Continue to make and spell **dug**, **hug**, **jug**, **mug**, **rug**, **tug**, **snug**, and **plug**.

4. Collect the Letter Cards

Call for each letter to review the letter names.

Lesson 25
Pattern: ub

Letters needed: **u, b, c, l, r, s,** and **t**

1. Books to Read

- *There's a Bug in My Mug*! by Kent Salisbury (McClanahan, 1997), ISBN 1-56293-931-9. This book is filled with two-line rhymes. Read the book; reread page 3 and talk about **ub** pattern in **tub** and **sub**.

- *Rub a Dub, Dub, Three Men in a Tub*, found in any collection of nursery rhymes. Read the rhyme and talk about the **ub** pattern in **rub** and **tub**.

2. Making Words: Blend and segment to read words

First, make the pattern **ub** with the letter card children. Lead the children to say the letter sounds and pattern **u/b**, **ub**. Then make and read a word using one of the other letter cards (**t**) and ask, "Who can read this word?" Together with the class, blend the letter sounds and say **t/u/b**, **tub**. Use the word in a sentence: "The boy took his bath in a **tub**." Continue this way with the other letters to make and read **c/u/b**, **cub**; **r/u/b**, **rub**; and **s/u/b**, **sub.** Use two letter sounds together with the pattern to make and read the words **club** and **stub**.

3. Making Words: Blend and segment to spell words

After making and reading words, use the same letter cards and lead the class to spell words. Ask the class to point to the letter to put in front of **ub** to make the word **tub**. Continue to make and spell **cub**, **rub**, **sub**, **club**, and **stub**.

4. Collect the Letter Cards

Call for each letter to review the letter names.

Lesson 26
Pattern: un

Letters needed: **u**, **n**, **b**, **f**, **g**, **r**, and **s**

1. Book to Read

- *One Fish, Two Fish, Red Fish, Blue Fish* by Dr. Seuss (Random House, 1960, renewed 1988), ISBN 10: 0-375-84166-0. Read the book; reread page 10 and talk about the **un** pattern in **run**, **fun**, and **sun**.

2. Making Words: Blend and segment to read words

First, make the pattern **un** with the letter card children. Lead the children to say the letter sounds and pattern **u/n**, **un**. Then make and read a word using one of the other letter cards (**s**) and ask, "Who can read this word?" Together with the class, blend the letter sounds and say **s/u/n**, **sun**. Use the word in a sentence: "The **sun** is (not) hot today." Continue this way with the other letters to make and read **b/u/n**, **bun**; **f/u/n**, **fun**; **g/u/n**, **gun**; and **r/u/n**, **run**.

3. Making Words: Blend and segment to spell words

After making and reading words, use the same letter cards and lead the class to spell words. Ask the class to point to the letter to put in front of **un** to make the word **sun**. Continue to make and spell **bun**, **fun**, **gun**, and **run**.

4. Collect the Letter Cards

Call for each letter to review the letter names.

Lesson 27
Pattern: ut

Letters needed: **u, t, b, c, g, h, n, r,** and **s**

1. Book to Read

- *I Can Read with My Eyes Shut!* by Dr. Seuss (Random House, 1978), ISBN 0-394-83912-9. Read the book; reread page 28 and talk about the **ut** pattern in **Hut-Zut** and **shut**.

2. Making Words: Blend and segment to read words

First, make the pattern **ut** with the letter card children. Lead the children to say the letter sounds and pattern **u/t**, **ut**. Then make and read a word using one of the other letter cards (**n**) and ask, "Who can read this word?" Together with the class, blend the letter sounds and say **n-u-t/nut**. Use the word in a sentence: "I found a **nut** under the tree." Continue this way with the other letters to make and read **b/u/t**, **but;**, **c/u/t**, **cut**; **g/u/t**, **gut**; **h/u/t**, **hut**; and **r/u/t**, **rut**. (If you have taught the letter sound **sh**, make and read the word **shut**.)

3. Making Words: Blend and segment to spell words

After making and reading words, use the same letter cards and lead the class to spell words. Ask the class to point to the letter to put in front of **ut** to make the word **nut**. Continue to make and spell **but**, **cut**, **hut**, and **rut** (**shut**).

4. Collect the Letter Cards

Call for each letter to review the letter names.

Lesson 28
Pattern: ump

Letters needed: u, m, p (2), b, c, d, j, h, l, s, and t

1. Books to Read

- *The Cat in the Hat* by Dr. Seuss (Random House, 1957, renewed 1985), ISBN 0-394-80001-X. Read the book; reread page 5 and talk about the **ump** pattern in **bump** and **jump**.

- *One Fish, Two Fish, Red Fish, Blue Fish* by Dr. Seuss (Random House, 1960, renewed 1988), ISBN 10: 0-375-84166-0. Read the book; reread pages 18 and 19 and talk about the **ump** pattern in **bump**, **wump**, **hump**, **gump**, and **jump**.

- *Miss Spider's New Car* by David Kirk (Scholastic, 1997), ISBN 0-590-30713-4. Read the book; reread page 21 (page 10 of text) and talk about the **ump** pattern in **bump**, **pump**, and **jump**.

2. Making Words: Blend and segment to read words

First, make the pattern **ump** with the letter card children. Lead the children to say the letter sounds and pattern **u/m/p**, **ump**. Then make and read a word using one of the other letter cards (**j**) and ask, "Who can read this word?" Together with the class, blend the letter sounds and say **j/u/m/p**, **jump**. Use the word in a sentence: "I can **jump**." Continue this way with the other letters to make and read **b/u/m/p**, **bump**; **d/u/m/p**, **dump**; **h/u/m/p**, **hump**; **l/u/m/p**, **lump**; and **p/u/m/p**, **pump**. Use two letter sounds together with the pattern to make and read the words **plump** and **stump** (**thump**).

3. Making Words: Blend and segment to spell words

After making and reading words, use the same letter cards and lead the class to spell words. Ask the class to point to the letter to put in front of **ump** to make the word jump. Continue to make and spell **bump**, **dump**, **hump**, **lump**, **pump**, **plump**, and **stump** (**thump**).

4. Collect the Letter Cards

Call for each letter to review the letter names.

Lesson 29

Review Patterns:
ug, ub, un, ut, and ump

Letter cards needed for this review lesson: u, b, g, j, h, m, n, p, r, and t

Words to make (read and spell) together:

1. nut
2. hut
3. tub
4. rub
5. rug
6. bug
7. bun
8. run
9. jump
10. hump

For this review lesson have the children give you a sentence for each word they make.

After the lesson read or reread a book with one or more of these patterns in it for transfer.

Lesson 30
Pattern: ack

Letters needed: **a**, **c**, **k**, **b**, **j**, **l**, **m**, **p**, **r**, **s**, **t**, and **z**

1. Books to Read

- *Zoo Looking* by Mem Fox (Mondo, 1996), ISBN 1-57255-010-4. Read the book; it has words on every text page with the **ack** pattern in it! Talk about the sound those three letters make.

- *Down on the Farm* by Merrily Kutner (Holiday House, 2000), ISBN 0-8234-1721-2. Read the book; reread page 11 and talk about the **ack** pattern in **back** and **quack.**

- *Hop on Pop* by Dr. Seuss (Random House, 1963, renewed 1991), ISBN 0-394-80029-X. Read the book; reread pages 48 through 51 and talk about the **ack** pattern in **back**, **black**, and **snack**.

2. Making Words: Blend and segment to read words

Make the pattern **ack** with the letter card children. Tell the children that the **c** and **k** make one sound. Lead the children to say the letter sounds and pattern **a/ck**, **ack**. Then make and read a word using one of the other letter cards (**b**) and ask, "Who can read this word?" Together with the class, blend the letter sounds and say **b/a/ck**, **back**. Use the word in a sentence: "Go to the **back** of the line." Continue this way with **J/a/ck**, **Jack**; **M/a/ck**, **Mack**; **p/a/ck**, **pack**; **r/a/ck**, **rack**; **s/a/ck**, **sack**; **t/a/ck**, **tack**; and **Z/a/ck**, **Zack**. Remember that the names **Jack**, **Mack**, and **Zack** need a capital letter. Use two letter sounds together with the pattern to make and read the words **black**, **smack**, **stack**, and **track**. (If you have taught the **sh** sound, add the word **shack.**)

3. Making Words: Blend and segment to spell words

Use the same letter cards and lead the class to spell some words. Ask the class to point to the letter to put in front of **ack** to make the words **back**, **Jack**, **Mack**, **sack**, **rack**, **tack**, **Zack**, **black**, **smack**, **stack**, and **track** (**shack**).

4. Collect the Letter Cards

Call for each letter to review the letter names.

Lesson 31
Pattern: and

Letters needed: a, n, d, b, h, l, r, s, and t

1. Books to Read

- *I'm Gonna Like Me: Letting Off a Little Self-Esteem* by Jamie Lee Curtis (Joanna Colter Books/HarperCollins, 2002), ISBN 0-06-028762-6. Read the book; reread page 9 and talk about the **and** pattern in **stand** and **hand**.

- *Alphababies* by Kim Golding (DK Publishing, 1998), ISBN 0-7894-2529-7. Read this alphabet book; reread pages 5 and 6 and talk about the **and** pattern in **grand** and **hand**.

- *Miss Spider's Tea Party* by David Kirk (Scholastic, 1994), ISBN 0-590-47724-2. Read the book; reread the fourth page of text and talk about the **and** pattern in the words **demand** and **hand**.

2. Making Words: Blend and segment to read words

First, make the pattern **and** with the letter card children. Lead the children to say the letter sounds and pattern **a/n/d, and**. Then make and read a word using one of the other letter cards (**h**) and ask, "Who can read this word?" Together with the class, blend the letter sounds and say **h/a/n/d, hand**. Use the word in a sentence: "Raise your **hand** if you know the answer." Continue this way with the other letters to make and read **b/a/n/d, band**; **l/a/n/d, land**; and **s/a/n/d, sand**. Use two letter sounds together with the pattern to make and read the words **brand** and **stand**.

3. Making Words: Blend and segment to spell words

After making and reading words, use the same letter cards and lead the class to spell words. Ask the class to point to the letter to put in front of **and** to make the word **hand.** Continue to make and spell **band**, **land**, **sand**, **brand**, and **stand.**

4. Collect the Letter Cards

Call for each letter to review the letter names.

Lesson 32
Pattern: end

Letters needed: e, n, d, b, l, m, s, and p

1. Books to Read

- *Boy, You're Amazing!* by Virginia Kroll (Albert Whitman, 2004), ISBN 0-8075-0868-3. Read the book; reread page 20 and listen for the **end** pattern in **friend** and **mend** on that page.

- *My Friends* by Taro Gomi (Cronicle Books, 1990), ISBN 0-02-179092-2. Read the book; reread several pages, having the children listen for the word **friend**, then talk about the **end** pattern.

- *Animal A B Cs* by Susan Hood (Troll, 1995), ISBN 0-8167-3572-7. Read this ABC book; reread page Uu and talk about the **end** pattern in **friend** and **pretend**.

2. Making Words: Blend and segment to read words

First, make the pattern **end** with the letter card children. Lead the children to say the letter sounds and pattern **e/n/d**, **end.** Then make and read a word using one of the other letter cards (**b**) and ask, "Who can read this word?" Together with the class, blend the letter sounds and say **b/e/n/d**, **bend**. Use the word in a sentence: "Who can **bend** down and touch their toes?" Continue this way with the other letters to make and read **l/e/n/d**, **lend**; **m/e/n/d**, **mend**; and **s/e/n/d**, **send**. Use two letter sounds together with the pattern to make and read the words **blend** and **spend**.

3. Making Words: Blend and segment to spell words

After making and reading words, use the same letter cards and lead the class to spell words. Ask the class to point to the letter to put in front of **end** to make the word **bend.** Continue to make and spell **lend**, **mend**, **send**, **blend**, and **spend.**

4. Collect the Letter Cards

Call for each letter to review the letter names.

Lesson 33
Pattern: ent

Letters needed: e, n, t, b, d, p, t, r, s, v, and w

1. Books to Read

- *My Grandpa and I* by P. K. Hallinan (Candy Cane Press, 2002), ISBN 0-82494-219-1. Read the book; reread the page with the **ent** pattern and talk about the **ent** pattern in **tent** and **went**.

- *The Night Before Summer Vacation* by Natasha Wing (Grosset and Dunlap, 2002), ISBN 0-448-42830-X. Read the book; reread the pages with the **ent** pattern and talk about the **ent** in **went** and **tent**.

- *Hop on Pop* by Dr. Seuss (Random House, 1963, renewed 1991), ISBN: 0-394-80029-X. Read the book; reread page 53 and listen for the **ent** pattern in **went**, **tent**, **sent**, and **tent**.

2. Making Words: Blend and segment to read words

First, make the pattern **ent** with the letter card children. Lead the children to say the letter sounds and pattern **e/n/t**, **ent**. Then make and read a word using one of the other letter cards (**w**) and ask, "Who can read this word?" Together with the class, blend the letter sounds and say **w/e/n/t**, **went**. Use the word in a sentence: "I **went** to the store with my friend." Continue this way with the other letters to make and read **b/e/n/t**, **bent**; **d/e/n/t**, **dent**; **t/e/n/t**, **tent**; **r/e/n/t**, **rent**; **s/e/n/t**, **sent**; and **v/e/n/t**, **vent**. Use two letter sounds together with the pattern to make and read the words **Brent**, **spent**, and **Trent**. Remember to use and talk about the capital letter used for names.

3. Making Words: Blend and segment to spell words

After making and reading words, use the same letter cards and lead the class to spell words. Ask the class to point to the letter to put in front of **ent** to make the word **went**. Continue to make and spell **bent**, **dent**, **tent**, **sent**, **rent**, **vent**, **Brent**, **spent**, and **Trent**.

4. Collect the Letter Cards

Call for each letter to review the letter names.

Lesson 34
Pattern: ing

Letters needed: i, n, g, b, k, r, s, t, and w

1. Books to Read

- *I'm Gonna Like Me: Letting Off a Little Self-Esteem* by Jamie Lee Curtis (Joanna Colter Books/HarperCollins, 2002), ISBN: 0-06-028762-6. Read the book; reread page 17 and talk about the **ing** pattern in **thing** and **ring**.

- *One Fish, Two Fish, Red Fish, Blue Fish* by Dr. Seuss (Random House, 1960, renewed 1988), ISBN 13: 978-0-375-84166-0. Read the book; reread page 40 and talk about the **ing** pattern in **Ying**, **sing**, and **anything**.

- *Miss Bindergarten Celebrates the 100th Day of Kindergarten* by Joseph Slate (Dutton Children's Books, 1998), ISBN 0-525-46000-4. Read the book; reread page 2 and talk about the **ing** pattern in **bring** and **thing**.

2. Making Words: Blend and segment to read words

Make the pattern **ing** with the letter card children. Tell the children they cannot blend these letter sounds together; when **ing** is at the end of a word, just say **ing**. Then make and read a word using one of the other letter cards (**s**) and ask, "Who can read this word?" Together with the class, blend the letter sounds and say **s/ing**, **sing**. Use the word in a sentence: "I can **sing** that song." Continue this way with the other ther letters to make and read **B/ing**, **Bing**; **d/ing**, **ding**; **k/ing**, **king**; **r/ing**, **ring**; and **w/ing**, **wing**. Remember the capital letter for the name **Bing**. Use two letter sounds together with the pattern to make and read the words **bring**, **sting**, and **swing**. (If you have taught the **th** sound, make **thing**.)

3. Making Words: Blend and segment to spell words

After making and reading words, use the same letter cards and lead the class to spell words. Ask the class to point to the letter to put in front of **ing** to make the word **sing**. Continue to make and spell **Bing**, **ding**, **king**, **ring**, **wing**, **bring**, **sting**, and **swing** (**thing**).

4. Collect the Letter Cards

Call for each letter to review the letter names.

Lesson 35
Pattern: ink

Letters needed: **i**, **n**, **k**, **b**, **d**, **p**, **l**, **m**, **r**, **s**, **t**, and **w**

1. Books to Read

- *Ten Apples Up on Top* by Theo LeSieg (Random House, 1961), ISBN 0-394-80019-2. Read the book; reread pages 31 through 33 and talk about the **ink** pattern in the words **think** and **drink**.

- *One Fish, Two Fish, Red Fish, Blue Fish* by Dr. Seuss (Random House, 1960, renewed 1988), ISBN 10: 0-375-84166-0. Read the book; reread pages 42 and 43 and talk about the **ink** pattern in **wink**, **drink**, **pink**, **ink**, **Yink**, and **think**.

- *Sheep in a Shop* by Nancy Shaw (Houghton Mifflin, 1991, renewed 1996), ISBN 0-395-73329-4. Read the book; reread page 24 and talk about the **ink** pattern in **blink** and **think**.

- *Loud Lips Lucy* by Tolya L. Thompson (Savoy Publishing House, 2002), ISBN 0-970896-0-4. Read the book; reread page 15 and talk about the **ink** pattern in **think** and **sink**.

2. Making Words: Blend and segment to read words

Make the **ink** pattern with the letter card children. Tell the children they cannot blend these letter sounds together; when it is at the end of a word, just say **ink**. Then make and read a word using one of the other letter cards (**s**) and ask, "Who can read this word?" Together with the class, blend the letter sounds and say **s/ink**, **sink**. Use the word in a sentence: "A rock will **sink** in water." Continue this way with the other letters to make and read **p/ink**, **pink**; **l/ink**, **link**; **m/ink**, **mink**; **r/ink**, **rink**; and **w/ink**, **wink**. Use two letter sounds together with the pattern to make and read **blink**, **drink**, and **stink** (**think**).

3. Making Words: Blend and segment to spell words

After making and reading words, use the letter cards and lead the class to spell words. Ask the class to point to the letter to put with **ink** to make the word **sink**. Continue to make and spell **pink**, **link**, **mink**, **rink**, **wink**, **blink**, **drink**, and **stink** (**think**).

4. Collect the Letter Cards

Call for each letter to review the letter names.

Letter 36

Pattern: ank

Letters needed: a, n, k, b, d, h, l, r, s, and t

1. Books to Read

- *Madeline* by Ludwig Bemelmans (Puffin Penguin Books, 1939, renewed in 1967), ISBN 0-14-050-198-3. Read the book; reread page 24 and talk about the **ank** pattern in **drank** and **crank.**

- *Sheep in a Shop* by Nancy Shaw (Houghton Mifflin, 1991, renewed 1996), ISBN 0-395-73329-4. Read the book; reread page 22 and talk about the **ank** pattern in **bank** and **clank.**

2. Making Words: Blend and segment to read words

Make the pattern **ank** with the letter card children. Tell the children they cannot blend these letter sounds together; when it is at the end of a word, just say **ank**. Then make and read a word using one of the other letter cards (**b**) and ask, "Who can read this word?" Together with the class, blend the letter sounds and say **b/ank**, **bank**. Use the word in a sentence: "I save my money at the **bank**." Continue this way with the other letters to make and read **H/ank**, **Hank**; **r/ank**, **rank**; and **s/ank**, **sank**. Remember the capital letter for the name **Hank**. Use two letter sounds together with the pattern to make and read the words **blank** and **drank**. (If you have taught the **th** sound, make and read **thank**.)

3. Making Words: Blend and segment to spell words

After making and reading words, use the same letter cards and lead the class to spell words. Ask the class to point to the letter to put in front of **ank** to make the word **bank**. Continue to make and spell **Hank**, **rank**, **sank**, **blank**, and **drank** (**thank**).

4. Collect the Letter Cards

Call for each letter to review the letter names.

Lesson 37
Pattern: unk

Letters needed: **u, n, k** (2), **b, d, j, h, s** and **t**

1. Books to Read

- *My Nose Is a Hose!* by Kent Salisbury (McClanahan, 1997), ISBN 1-56293-930-0. Read this book of two lined rhymes; reread page 9 and talk about the **unk** pattern in **trunk** and **skunk**.

- *The Library* by Sarah Stewart (Farrar, Straus, and Giroux, 1999), ISBN 0-37444-394-7. Read the book; reread the page with the **unk** pattern in **trunk** and **bunk**.

2. Making Words: Blend and segment to read words

First, make the pattern **unk** with the letter card children. Tell the children they cannot blend these letter sounds together; when it is at the end of a word, just say **unk**. Have them say **unk** with you. Then make and read a word using one of the other letter cards (**b**) and ask, "Who can read this word?" Together with the class, blend the letter sounds and say **b/unk**, **bunk**. Use the word in a sentence: "I will sleep on the **bunk**." Continue this way with the other letters to make and read **d/unk**, **dunk**; **h/unk**, **hunk**; **j/unk**, **junk**; and **s/unk**, **sunk**. Use two letter sounds together with the pattern to make and read the words **skunk** and **stunk**. (If you have taught the **ch** sound, make and read the word **chunk**.)

3. Making Words: Blend and segment to spell words

After making and reading words, use the same letter cards and lead the class to spell words. Ask the class to point to the letter to put in front of **unk** to make the word **bunk**. Continue to make and spell **dunk**, **hunk**, **junk**, **sunk**, **skunk**, and **stunk** (**chunk**).

4. Collect the Letter Cards

Call for each letter to review the letter names.

Lesson 38

Review Patterns:
ack, and, end, ent, ing, and ink

Letters needed: a, e, i, b, c, d, k, n, p, s, and t

Words to make (read and spell) together:

1. back
2. pack
3. pink
4. sink
5. sing
6. bent
7. bend
8. send
9. sent
10. sand

For this review lesson have the children give you a sentence for each word they make.

After the lesson read or reread a book with one or more of these patterns in it for transfer.

Lesson 39
Pattern: ay

Letters needed: **a**, **y**, **b**, **c**, **d**, **f**, **h**, **l**, **k**, **m**, **p**, **r**, **s**, **t**, and **w**

1. Books to Read

- *Annie Bananie* by Leah Komaiko (Scholastic, 1987), ISBN 0-590-42844-6. Read the book; reread pages 8 and 9 and talk about the **ay** pattern in **play** and **away**. On page 18 talk about the **ay** pattern in **away** and **birthday**.

- *Miss Spider's Tea Party* by David Kirk (Scholastic, 1994), ISBN 0-590-47724-2. Read the book; reread page 4, and talk about the **ay** pattern in the words **May**, **day**, **stay**, and **away**.

- *The Cat in the Hat* by Dr. Seuss (Random House, 1957, renewed 1985), ISBN 0-394-80001-X. Read the book; reread pages 1, 37, and 60 and point out the **ay** pattern in **play** and **day**.

2. Making Words: Blend and segment to read words

First, make the pattern **ay** with the letter card children. Explain that you can't hear the **y** sound; you can hear only the letter **a** saying its name. Have the children say the **ay** sound with you. Then, make and read a word using one of the other letter cards (**d**) and ask, "Who can read this word?" Together with the class, blend the letter sounds and say **d/ay**, **day**. Use the word in a sentence: "What a nice (rainy) **day**." Continue this way with the other letters to make and read **h/ay**, **hay**; **F/ay**, **Fay**; **J/ay**, **Jay**; **K/ay**, **Kay**; **l/ay**, **lay**; **m/ay**, **may**; **R/ay**, **Ray**; **s/ay**, **say**; and **w/ay**, **way**. Remember to use and talk about the capital letters for names. Use two letter sounds together with the pattern to make and read the words **clay**, **play**, and **stay**.

3. Making Words: Blend and segment to spell words

After making and reading words, use the same letter cards and lead the class to spell words. Ask the class to point to the letter to put in front of **ay** to make the word **day**. Continue to make and spell **hay**, **Fay**, **Jay**, **Kay**, **lay**, **may**, **Ray**, **say**, **way**, **clay**, **play**, and **stay**.

4. Collect the Letter Cards

Call for each letter to review the letter names.

Lesson 40
Pattern: ake

Letters needed: **a**, **e**, **k**, **b**, **c**, **f**, **j**, **l**, **m**, **r**, **t**, and **w**

1. Books to Read

- *Jake Baked the Cake* by B. G. Hennessy (Puffin Books, 1992). Read the book; have the children listen as you reread the refrain on any of several pages, "While **Jake baked** the **cake.**" Talk about the **ake** pattern.

- *Hunky Dory Ate I* by Katie Evans (Puffin Unicorn Books, 1992), ISBN 014055856X, 978-0140558562. Read the book; reread the first two sentences in the book, "Clara **Lake baked** a **cake**. Hunky Dory Ate It!" and talk about the **ake** pattern in **Lake**, **baked**, and **cake**.

- *I Can Read with My Eyes Shut!* by Dr. Seuss (Random House, 1978), ISBN 0007158513, 978-0007158515. Read the book; reread page 19 and talk about the **ake** pattern in **Jake** and **Snake**.

2. Making Words: Blend and segment letter sounds to read words

Using the letter card children, make **ake**. Explain that you can't hear the **e** sound; you can hear only the **a** saying its name and **k** in this pattern. We call this a silent **e**. (Have the letter card child with the **e** put his or her hand over his or her mouth.) Have the children say the **ake** sound with you. Put the child with the letter card **b** in front of the three children wearing **ake**. Ask the children to read this word. Lead the class to say **b/ake**, **bake.** Use the word in a sentence: "I like to **bake** cookies." Then make and read some other words: **c/ake**, **cake**; **f/ake**, **fake**; **J/ake**, **Jake**; **m/ake**, **make**; **l/ake**, **lake**; **r/ake**, **rake**; **t/ake**, **take**; and **w/ake**, **wake**. Remember the capital letter needed for **Jake**. Use two letter sounds together with the pattern to make and read the words **Blake**, **brake**, and **flake** (**shake**)**.**

3. Making Words: Blend and segment letter sounds to spell words

Using the three letter cards **ake**, ask the children to point to the letter needed to make the word **bake**. When they point to the letter child **b**, have them say **b/ake**, **bake**. Then follow the same procedure to make and spell **cake**, **fake**, **Jake**, **make**, **lake**, **rake**, **take**, **wake**, **Blake**, **brake**, and **flake** (**shake**).

4. Collect the Letter Cards

Call for each letter to review the letter names.

Lesson 41
Pattern: ate

Letters needed: **a, e, t, d, h, l, k, m, k, p, r** and **s**

1. Books to Read

- *The Wedding* by Eve Bunting (Charlesbridge, 2005), ISBN 1-58089-040-7. Read the book; reread page 8 and talk about the **ate** pattern in **gate** and **late** and in **date** and **late**.

- *The Library* by Sarah Stewart (Farrar, Straus, and Giroux, 1999), ISBN 0-37444-394-7. Read the book; reread the pages with the **ate** pattern and talk about the **ate** pattern in **skate** and **rate** and in **date** and **late**.

- *Counting Is for the Birds* by Frank Mazzola Jr. (Charlesbridge, 1997), ISBN 0-88106-950-7. Read the book; reread the page with the **ate** pattern and talk about the pattern in **mate** and **rate**.

2. Making Words: Blend and segment letter sounds to read words

Using the letter card children, make **ate**. Explain that you can't hear the **e** sound; you can hear only the **a** saying its name and **t** in this pattern. We call this a silent **e**. (Have the letter card child with the **e** put his or her hand over his or her mouth.) Have the children say the **ate** sound with you. Put the child with the letter card **d** in front of the three children wearing **ate**. Ask the children to read this word. Lead the class to say **d/ate, date.** Use the word in a sentence: "Today's **date** is the fifth of March." Then make and read some other words: **g/ate, gate; h/ate, hate; m/ate, mate; l/ate, late;** and **K/ate, Kate.** Remember the capital letter needed for **Kate.** Use two letter sounds together with the pattern to make and read the words **plate** and **skate.**

3. Making Words: Blend and segment letter sounds to spell words

Using the three letter cards **ate**, ask the children to point to the letter needed to make the word **date**. When they point to the letter child **d**, have them say **d/ate, date**. Then follow the same procedure to make and spell **gate, hate, Kate, mate, late, plate,** and **skate.**

4. Collect the Letter Cards

Call for each letter to review the letter names.

Lesson 42

Pattern: ame

Letters needed: a, e, m, b, c, g, l, n, f, s, and t

1. Books to Read

- *Loud Lips Lucy* by Tolya L. Thompson (Savoy, 2002), ISBN 0-970896-0-4. Read the book; reread page 10 and talk about the **ame** pattern in **name** and **same**.

- *The Brand New Kid* by Katie Couric, illustrated by Marjorie Priceman (Doubleday, a division of Random House, 2000), ISBN 0-385-50030-0. Read the book; reread page 11 and talk about the **ame** pattern in **game** and **name**.

- *The Night Before Summer Vacation* by Natasha Wing (Grosset & Dunlap, 2002), ISBN 0-448-42830-X. Read the book; reread the page with the **ame** pattern and talk about it in **came** and **game**.

2. Making Words: Blend and segment letter sounds to read words

Using the letter card children, make **ame**. Explain that you can't hear the **e** sound; you can hear only the **a** saying its name and **m** in this pattern. We call this a silent **e**. (Have the letter card child with the **e** put his or her hand over his or her mouth.) Have the children say the **ame** sound with you. Put the child with the letter card **n** in front of the three children wearing **ame**. Ask the children to read this word. Lead the class to say **n/ame**, **name**. Use the word in a sentence: "What is your **name**?" Then make and read some other words: **c/ame**, **came**; **g/ame**, **game**; **f/ame**, **fame**; **s/ame**, **same**; and **t/ame**, **tame**. Use two letter sounds together with the pattern to make and read the words **blame** and **flame**. (If you have taught the **sh** pattern, then add **shame**.)

3. Making Words: Blend and segment letter sounds to spell words

Using the three letter cards **ame**, ask the children to point to the letter needed to make the word **name**. When they point to the letter child **n**, have them say **n/ame**, **name**. Then follow the same procedure to make and spell **came**, **fame**, **game**, **same**, **tame**, **blame**, and **flame** (**shame**).

4. Collect the Letter Cards

Call for each letter to review the letter names.

Lesson 43
Pattern: ide

Letters needed: **i**, **e**, **d**, **b**, **g**, **h**, **l**, **r**, **s**, **t**, and **w**

1. Books to Read

- *Inside, Outside, Upside Down* by Stan and Jan Berenstain (Random House, 1968, renewed 1997), ISBN 0-679-88632-X. Read the book; talk about the **ide** pattern in the title words **inside**, **outside**, and **upside**.

- *I Can Read with My Eyes Shut!* by Dr. Seuss (Random House, 1978), ISBN 0-394-83912-9. Read the book; reread the last page and talk about the **ide** pattern in **wide** and **side**.

- *Lunch Money and Other Poems About School* by Carol Diggory Shields (Puffin Penguin Books, 1995), ISBN 0-525-45345-8. Read the poem on pages 22 and 23 and talk about the **ide** pattern in **slide** and **outside**.

2. Making Words: Blend and segment letter sounds to read words

Using the letter card children, make **ide**. Explain that you can't hear the **e** sound; you can hear only the **i** and **d** in this pattern. We call this a silent **e**. (Have the letter card child with the **e** put his or her hand over his or her mouth.) Have the children say the **ide** sound with you. Put the child with the letter card **h** in front of the three children wearing **ide**. Ask the children to read this word. Lead the class to say **h/ide**, **hide**. Use the word in a sentence: "It is your turn to **hide**." Then make and read some other words: **r/ide**, **ride**; **s/ide**, **side**; **t/ide**, **tide**; and **w/ide**, **wide**. Use two letter sounds together with the pattern to make and read the words **bride**, **glide**, and **slide**.

3. Making Words: Blend and segment letter sounds to spell words

Using the three letter cards **ide**, ask the children to point to the letter needed to make the word **hide**. When they point to the letter child **h**, have them say **h/ide**, **hide**. Then follow the same procedure to make and spell **ride**, **tide**, **side**, **bride**, **glide**, and **slide**.

4. Collect the Letter Cards

Call for each letter to review the letter names.

Lesson 44

Pattern: ine

Letters needed: **i**, **e**, **n**, **d**, **f**, **l**, **m**, **n** (2), **p**, and **v**

1. Books to Read

- *Madeline* by Ludwig Bemelmans (Puffin Books, 1939, renewed 1967), ISBN 0-14-050-198-3. Read the book; reread pages 9 through 12 and talk about the **ine** pattern in **nine**, **shine**, and **Madeline**.

- *Madeline in London* by Ludwig Bemelmans (Puffin Books, 1939, renewed 1977), ISBN 0-14-056649-X. Read the book; reread page 12 and talk about the **ine** pattern in **fine** and **line**.

- *Miss Spider's New Car* by David Kirk (Scholastic, 1997), ISBN 0-590-30713-4. Read the book; reread page 6 and let the class listen to the **ine** pattern in **divine**, **shine**, and **fine**.

2. Making Words: Blend and segment letter sounds to read words

Using the letter card children, make **ine**. Explain that you can't hear the **e** sound; you can hear only the **i** and **n** in this pattern. We call this a silent **e**. (Have the letter card child with the **e** put his or her hand over his or her mouth.) Have the children say the **ine** sound with you. Put the child with the letter card **f** in front of the three children wearing **ine**. Ask the children to read this word. Lead the class to say **f/ine**, **fine.** Use the word in a sentence: "I feel **fine**." Then make and read **d/ine**, **dine**; **l/ine**, **line**; **m/ine**, **mine**; **n/ine**, **nine**; **p/ine**, **pine**; and **v/ine**, **vine.** (If your students know the **sh** sound, have them read and spell **shine.**)

3. Making Words: Blend and segment letter sounds to spell words

Using the three letter cards **ine**, ask the children to point to the letter needed to make the word **fine**. When they point to the letter child **f**, have them say **f/ine**, **fine**. Then follow the same procedure to make and spell **dine**, **line**, **mine**, **nine**, **pine**, and **vine** (**shine**).

4. Collect the Letter Cards

Call for each letter to review the letter names.

Lesson 45
Pattern: eat

Letters needed: a, e, t, b, h, m, n, s, t and r

1. Books to Read

- *How I Spent My Summer Vacation* by Mark Teague (Dragonfly Books, 1996), ISBN 0-517-517-59999-8. Read the book; reread page 23 and talk about the **eat** pattern in **eat** and b**eat**.

- *How Many, How Many, How Many* by Rick Walton (Candlewick Press, 1996), ISBN 1-56402-656-6. Read the book; reread the page with the **eat** pattern and talk about the **eat** pattern in s**eat** and **eat**.

2. Making Words: Blend and segment letter sounds to read words

Using the letter card children, make **eat**. Explain that you can't hear the **a** sound; you can hear only the **e** saying its name and **t** in this pattern. We call this a silent **a**. (Have the letter card child with the **a** put his or her hand over his or her mouth.) Have the children say the **eat** sound with you. Put the child with the letter card **m** in front of the three children wearing **eat**. Ask the children to read this word. Lead the class to say **m/eat**, **meat.** Use the word in a sentence: "I (don't) eat **meat.**" Then make and read **b/eat**, **beat**; **h/eat**, **heat**; **n/eat**, **neat**; and **s/eat**, **seat.** Use two letters for the beginning sound and have them make and read **treat** (**cheat**).

3. Making Words: Blend and segment letter sounds to spell words

Using the three letter cards **eat**, ask the children to point to the letter needed to make the word **meat.** When they point to the letter child **m**, have them say **m/eat**, **meat.** Then follow the same procedure to make and spell **beat**, **heat**, **neat**, **seat**, and **treat**, (**cheat**).

4. Collect the Letter Cards

Call for each letter to review the letter names.

Lesson 46
Pattern: eep

Letters needed: e (2), p , b, d, j, k, l, s, t, and w

1. Books to Read

- *Down on the Farm* by Merrily Kutner, illustrated by Will Hillenbrand (Holiday House, 2000), ISBN 0-8234-1721-2. Read the book; reread page 23 and talk about the **eep** pattern in **sleep** and **peep**.

- *Alphababies* by Kim Golding (DK Publishing, 1998), ISBN 0-7894-2529-7. Read this book; reread pages 13 and 14 and talk about the **eep** pattern in **deep** and **sleep.**

- *Who's in the Shed?* by Brenda Parkes, illustrated by Ester Kasepuu (Rigby, 1986), ISBN 0-7312-0028-4. Read the book; reread pages 4 and 5 and talk about the **eep** pattern in **peep** and **sheep**.

- *Little Bo Peep*, found in any collection of nursery rhymes. Read the rhyme and talk about the **eep** in **Peep** and **sheep**.

2. Making Words: Blend and segment letter sounds to read words

Using the letter card children, make **eep**. Explain that you can't hear both the **e**'s in this pattern; you can hear only the **e** saying its name and the **p**. Have the children say **eep** with you. Put the child with the letter card **b** in front of the three children wearing **eep**. Ask the children to read this word. Lead the class to say **b/eep**, **beep**. Use the word in a sentence: "The horn on the car went **beep**." Then make and read **d/eep**, **deep**; **j/eep**, **jeep**; **k/eep**, **keep**; and **w/eep**, **weep**. Use two letters for the beginning sound and have them make and read **steep** and **sweep** (**sheep**).

3. Making Words: Blend and segment letter sounds to spell words

Using the three letter cards **eep**, ask the children to point to the letter needed to make the word **beep**. When they point to the letter child **b**, have them say **b/eep**, **beep**. Then follow the same procedure to make and spell **deep**, **jeep**, **keep**, **weep**, **steep**, and **sweep** (**sheep**).

4. Collect the Letter Cards

Call for each letter to review the letter names.

Lesson 47
Pattern: ar

Letters needed: a, r, b, c, f, j, s, and t

1. Books to Read

- *The Brand New Kid* by Katie Couric (Doubleday, a division of Random House, 2000), ISBN 0-385-50030-0. Read the book; reread page 17 and talk about the **ar** pattern in **car** and **far**.
- *One Fish, Two Fish, Red Fish, Blue Fish* by Dr. Seuss (Random House, 1960, renewed 1988), ISBN 10: 0-375-84166-0. Read the book; reread page 4 and talk about the **ar** pattern in **star** and **car**.
- *Madeline* by Ludwig Bemelmans (Puffin Penguin Books, 1939, renewed 1967), ISBN 0-14-050-198-3. Read the book; reread page 33 and talk about the **ar** pattern in **far** and **scar**.

2. Making Words: Blend and segment to read words

Make the pattern **ar** with the letter card children. Explain when **a** and **r** are together, you can't hear the **a** sound; you can hear only the letter **r** saying its name. Have the class say the **ar** sound with you. Then make and read a word using one of the other letter cards (**c**) and ask, "Who can read this word?" Together with the class, blend the letter sounds and say **c/ar**, **car**. Use the word in a sentence: "I like my **car**." Continue this way with the other letters to make and read **b/ar**, **bar**; **f/ar**, **far**; **j/ar**, **jar**; and **t/ar**, **tar**. Using two letter sounds together, make and read the words **scar** and **star**.

3. Making Words: Blend and segment to spell words

After making and reading words, use the same letter cards and lead the class to spell words. Ask the class to point to the letter to put in front of **ar** to make the word **car**. Continue to make and spell **bar**, **far**, **jar**, **tar**, **scar**, and **star**.

4. Collect the Letter Cards

Call for each letter to review the letter names.

Lesson 48
Pattern: all

Letters needed: **a**, **l** (2), **b**, **c**, **f**, **h**, **m**, **s**, **t**, and **w**

1. Books to Read

- *The Cat in the Hat* by Dr. Seuss (Random House 1957, renewed 1985), ISBN 0-394-80001-X. Read the book; reread page 40 and have the children listen for the **all** pattern in **hall**, **wall**, **wall**, and **hall** on this page.

- *Hop on Pop* by Dr. Seuss (Random House 1963, renewed 1991), ISBN 0-394-80029-X. Read pages 8 through 11, listening for the **all** pattern in the words **all**, **tall, small**, **ball**, **wall**, and **fall**.

- *Today I Feel Silly and Other Moods that Make My Day* by Jamie Lee Curtis (Joanna Cotler Books/HarperCollins, 1998), ISBN 0-06-024560-3. Read the book; reread page 18 and talk about the **all** pattern in **small** and **call**.

2. Making Words: Blend and segment to read words

Make the pattern **all** with the letter card children. Explain that you can't blend these letter sounds together; you just say **all**. Have the children say the **all** sound with you. Then make and read a word using one of the other letter cards (**b**) and ask, "Who can read this word?" Together with the class, blend the letter sounds and say **b/all**, **ball**. Use the word in a sentence: "I like to play **ball** with my friends." Continue this way with the other letters to make and read **c/all**, **call**; **f/all**, **fall**; **h/all**, **hall**; **m/all**, **mall**; **t/all/tall**; and **w/all**, **wall**. Use two letter sounds together with the pattern to make and read the words **small** and **stall.**

3. Making Words: Blend and segment to spell words

After making and reading words, use the same letter cards and lead the class to spell words. Ask the class to point to the letter to put in front of **all** to make the word **ball**. Continue to make and spell **call**, **fall**, **hall**, **mall**, **tall**, **wall**, **small**, and **stall.**

4. Collect the Letter Cards

Call for each letter to review the letter names.

Lesson 49
Pattern: ook

Letters needed: o (2), **k, b, c, h, l, t,** and **r**

1. Books to Read

- *The Brand New Kid* by Katie Couric, illustrated by Marjorie Priceman (Doubleday, a division of Random House, 2000), ISBN 0-385-50030-0. Read the book; reread page 5 and talk about the **ook** pattern in **book** and **look**.

- *Miss Spider's Tea Party* by David Kirk (Scholastic, 1994), ISBN 0-590-47724-2. Read the book; reread the fifth page of text and talk about the **ook** pattern in **look** and **nook**.

- *One Fish, Two Fish, Red Fish, Blue Fish* by Dr. Seuss (Random House, 1960, renewed 1988), ISBN 10: 0-375-84166-0. Read the book; reread pages 30 and 31 and talk about the **ook** pattern in **hook**, **book**, **cook**, and **look**.

2. Making Words: Blend and segment to read words

Make the pattern **ook** with the letter card children. Explain that you can't blend these letters together; you just say **ook**. Have the children say **ook** with you. Then make and read a word using one of the other letter cards (**b**) and ask, "Who can read this word?" Together with the class, blend the letter sounds and say **b/ook**, **book**. Use the word in a sentence: "What is your favorite **book**?" Continue this way with the other letters to make and read **c/ook**, **cook**; **h/ook**, **hook**; **l-ook**, **look**; and **t/ook**, **took**. Use two letter sounds together with the pattern to make and read the words **brook** and **crook** (**shook**).

3. Making Words: Blend and segment to spell words

After making and reading words, use the same letter cards and lead the class to spell some words. Ask the class to point to the letter to put in front of **ook** to make the word **book**. Continue to make and spell **cook**, **hook**, **look**, **took**, **brook**, and **crook** (**shook**).

4. Collect the Letter Cards

Call for each letter to review the letter names.

Lesson 50

Review Patterns:
ake, ate, ame, ide, ine, and eat

Letters needed: a, e, i, d, l, k, l, m, n, s, and t

Words to make (read and spell) together:

1. make
2. take
3. Kate
4. tame
5. same
6. seat
7. meat
8. tide
9. side
10. dine

For this review lesson have the children give you a sentence for each word they make.

After the lesson read or reread a book with one or more of these patterns in it for transfer.

References

Adams, M. J. *Beginning to Read: Thinking and Learning about Print.* Cambridge, MA: MIT Press, 1990.

Cunningham, P. *Phonics They Use,* 1st ed. New York: HarperCollins, 1991.

Cunningham, P. *Phonics They Use,* 4th ed. Boston: Allyn and Bacon, 2005.

Cunningham, P. M., & Cunningham, J. W. "Making Words: Enhancing the Invented Spelling-Decoding Connection," *The Reading Teacher,* 46, 1992, pp. 106–107.

Cunningham, P. M., & Hall, D. P. *Making Words.* Torrance, CA: Good Apple, 1994.

Cunningham, P. M., & Hall, D. P. *Making More Words.* Torrance, CA: Good Apple, 1997.

Ehri, L. C., & Nunes, S. R. "The Role of Phonemic Awareness in Learning to Read," in A. E. Farstrup & S. J. Samuels (Eds.), *What Research Has to Say about Reading Instruction,* 3rd ed. Newark, DE: IRA, 2002.

Griffith, P., & Olson, M. "Phonemic Awareness Helps Beginning Readers Break the Code," *The Reading Teacher,* 45, 1992, pp. 516–523.

Hall, D. P., & Cunningham, P. M. *The Names Book: Using Names to Teach Reading, Writing, and Math in the Primary Grades.* Greensboro, NC: Carson-Dellarosa, 2003.

Hall, D. P., & Cunningham, P. M. *Month by Month Phonics for First Grade.* Greensboro, NC: Carson-Dellarosa, 1997, 2003.

Hall, D. P., & Cunningham, P. M. *Month by Month Reading, Writing, and Phonics in Kindergarten.* Greensboro, NC: Carson-Dellarosa, 1997, 2003.

Hall, D. P., & Williams, E. *Teacher's Guide to Building Blocks.* Greensboro, NC: Carson-Dellarosa, 2000.

National Reading Panel. *Teaching Children to Read: An Evidence-Based Assessment of the Scientific Research Literature on Reading and Its Implications for Reading Instruction: Reports of the Subgroups* (National Institute of Health Pub. No. 00-4754). Washington, DC: National Institute of Health, 2000.

Wylie, R. E., & Durrell, D. D. "Teaching Vowels through Phonograms," *Elementary English,* 47, pp. 787–791.

Yopp, H. K. "Developing Phonemic Awareness in Young Children," *The Reading Teacher,* 45, 1995, pp. 696–703.

Children's Books

Ahlberg, Janet, & Ahlberg, Allan. *Each Peach Pear Plum*. New York: Viking Press, Scholastic, 1978.

Arnold, Tedd. *More Parts*. New York: Puffin Books, 2005.

Babrera, Jane. *Old Mother Hubbard*. New York: Holiday House, 2001.

Beaumont, Karen. *I Ain't Gonna Paint No More!* New York: Harcourt, 2005.

Bemelmans, Ludwig. *Madeline*. New York: Puffin Penguin Books, 1939, renewed 1967.

Bemelmans, Ludwig. *Madeline in London*. New York: Puffin Books, 1939, renewed 1977.

Berenstain, Stan, & Berenstain, Jan. *Inside, Outside, Upside Down*. New York: Random House, 1968, 1997.

Bond, Felicia. *Tumble Bumble*. New York: Scholastic, 1996.

Bunting, Eve. *The Wedding*. Watertown, MA: Charlesbridge Publishing, 2005.

Couric, Katie. *The Brand New Kid*. New York: Doubleday, a division of Random House, 2000.

Curtis, Jamie Lee. *I'm Gonna Like Me: Letting Off a Little Self-Esteem*. New York: Joanna Colter Books/HarperCollins, 2002.

Curtis, Jamie Lee. *Today I Feel Silly and Other Moods that Make My Day*. New York: Joanna Cotler Books/HarperCollins Imprint, 1998.

Dr. Seuss. *The Cat in the Hat*. New York: Random House, 1957, renewed 1985.

Dr. Seuss. *Green Eggs and Ham*. New York: Random House, 1960.

Dr Seuss. *Hop on Pop*. New York: Random House, 1963, renewed 1991.

Dr. Seuss. *I Can Read with My Eyes Shut!* New York: Random House, 1978.

Dr. Seuss. *One Fish, Two Fish, Red Fish, Blue Fish*. New York: Random House,1960, renewed 1988.

Downey, Lynn. *The Flea's Sneeze*. New York: Henry Holt, 2000.

Eastman, Peter. *Fred and Ted Go Camping*. New York: Random House, 2005.

Edwards, Pamela Duncan. *The Grumpy Morning*. New York: Hyperion Books, 1998.

Evans, Katie. *Hunky Dory Ate It*. New York: Puffin Unicorn Books, 1992.

Fox, Mem. *Zoo Looking*. Greenvale, NY: Mondo Publishing, 1996.

Fred's Phonograms Series. Seattle, WA: I Knew That, Inc., 2001.

Golding, Kim. *Alphababies*. New York: DK Publishing, 1998.

Gomi, Taro. *My Friends/Mis Amigos*. San Francisco: Chronicle Books, 1990.

Hallinan, P. K. *My Grandpa and I*. Carmel, NY: Candy Cane Press, 2002.

Hennessy, B. G. *Jake Baked the Cake*. New York: Puffin Books, 1992.

Hood, Susan. *Animal A B Cs*. New York: Troll, 1995.

Jackson, Allison. *If the Shoe Fits*. New York: Henry Holt, 2001.

Kirk, David. *Miss Spider's New Car*. New York: Scholastic, 1997.

Kirk, David. *Miss Spider's Tea Party*. New York: Scholastic, 1995.

Komeiko, Leah. *Annie Bananie*. New York: Scholastic, 1987.

Kroll, Virginia. *Boy, You're Amazing!* Chicago: Albert Whitman, 2004.

Kutner, Merrily. *Down on the Farm*. New York: Holiday House, 2000.

Lillegard, Dee. *Hello School*. Shawnee, OK: Dragonfly Books, 2003.

Martin, Bill Jr. *Here Are My Hands*. New York: Henry Holt, 1989.

Mazzola, Frank, Jr. *Counting Is for the Birds*. Watertown, MA: Charlesbridge Publishing, 1997.

Parkes, Brenda. *Who's in the Shed?* Orlando, FL: Harcourt, 1986.

Pinczer, Elinor T. *Inchworm and a Half*. Boston: Houghton Mifflin, 2003.

Riley, Linnea. *Mouse Messu*. New York: Scholastic, 1997.

Salisbury, Kent. *My Nose is a Hose!* Kuttawa, NY: McClanahan, 1997.

Salisbury, Kent. *There's a Bug in My Mug*! Kuttawa, NY: McClanahan, 1997.

Shaw, Nancy. *Sheep in a Ship*. Boston: Houghton Mifflin, 1986.

Shaw, Nancy. *Sheep in a Shop*. Boston: Houghton Mifflin, 1991, 1996.

Shields, Carol Diggory. *Lunch Money and Other Poems About School*. New York: Puffin, 1995.

Slate, Joseph. *Miss Bindergarten Celebrates the 100th Day of Kindergarten*. New York: Dutton Children's Books, 1998.

Slate, Joseph. *Miss Bindergarten Stays Home from Kindergarten*. New York: Dutton Children's Books, 2000.

Smith, Annette. *The Three Billy Goats Gruff*. Orlando, FL: Rigby Publishers in the PM Traditional Tales and Plays Collection, 1997.

Stewart, Sarah. *The Library*. New York: Farrar, Straus, and Giroux, 1999.

Teague, Mark. *How I Spent My Summer Vacation*. Shawnee, OK: Dragonfly Books, 1995.

Thompson, Tolya L. *Loud Lips Lucy*. Manchester: Savoy, 2002.

Trussel-Cullen, Allen. *The Gingerbread Man.* Carlsbad, CA: Dominie Press, 1999.

Trussel-Cullen, Allen. *The Little Red Hen.* Carlsbad, CA: Dominie Press, 1999.

Trussell-Cullen, Allen. *The Three Little Pigs*. Carlsbad, CA: Dominie Press, 1999.

Walton, Rick. *How Many, How Many, How Many?* Cambridge, MA: Candlewick Press, 1996.

Wing, Natasha. *The Night Before Summer Vacation*. New York: Grosset and Dunlap, 2002.

Reproducible Letters

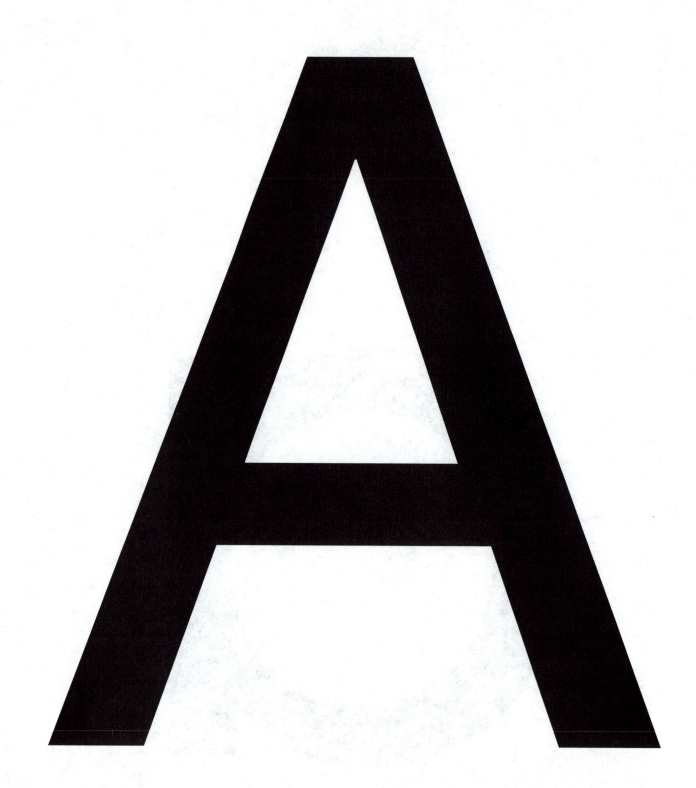

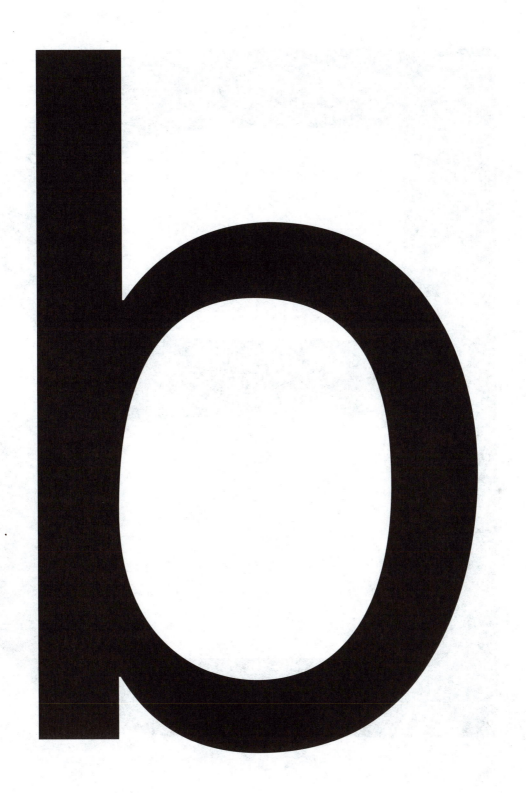

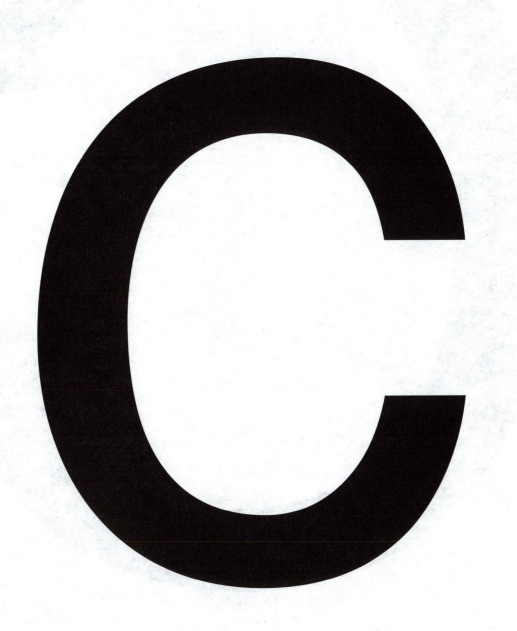

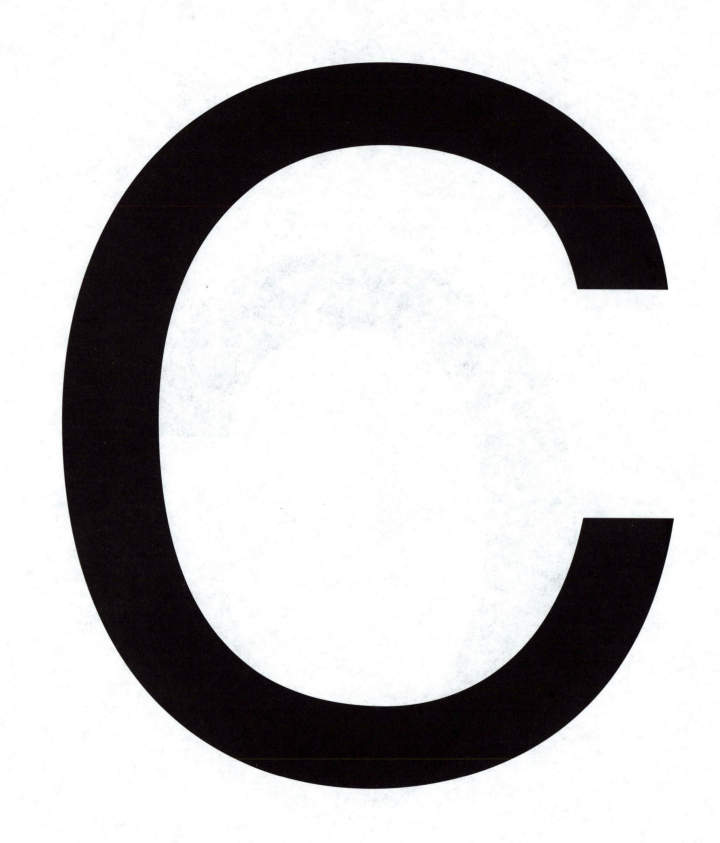

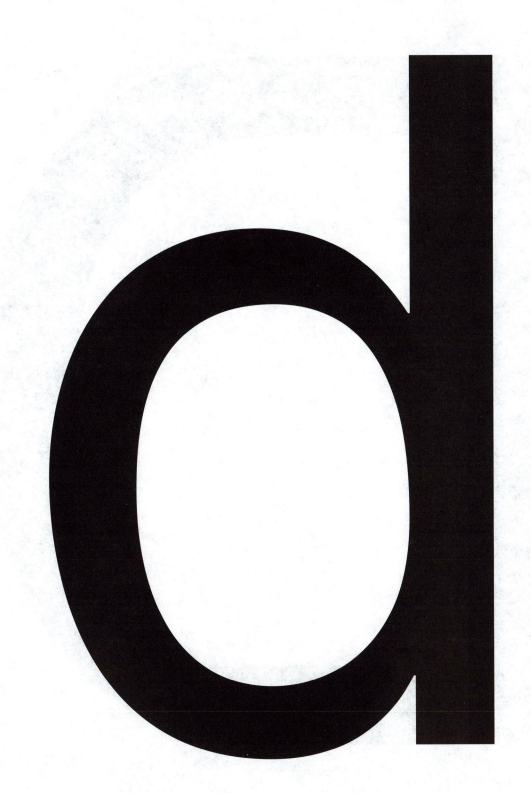

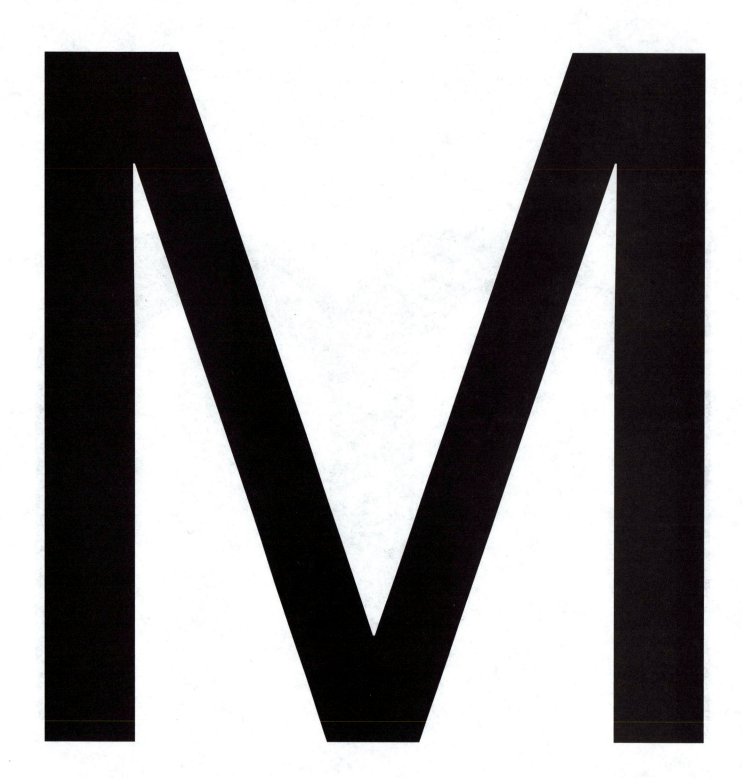

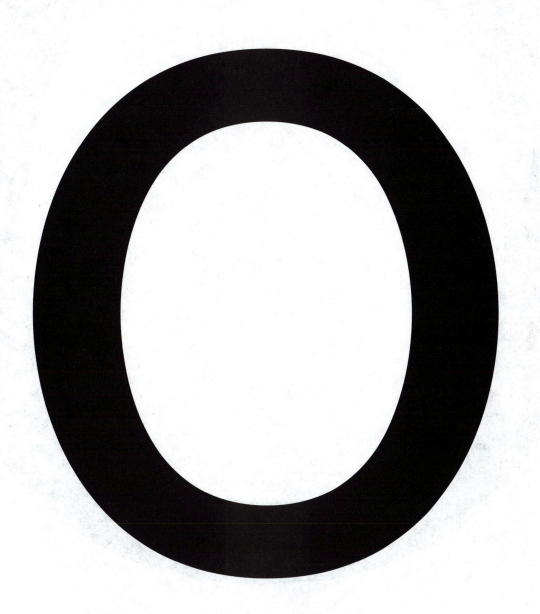

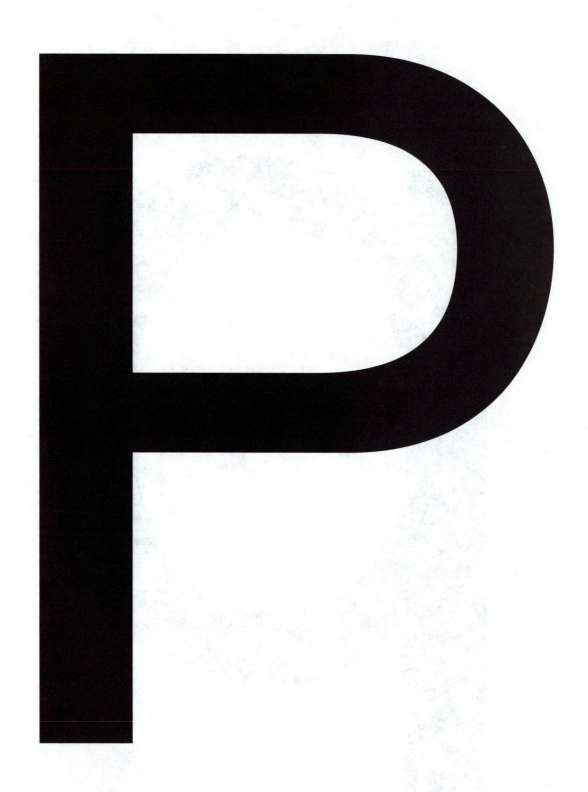

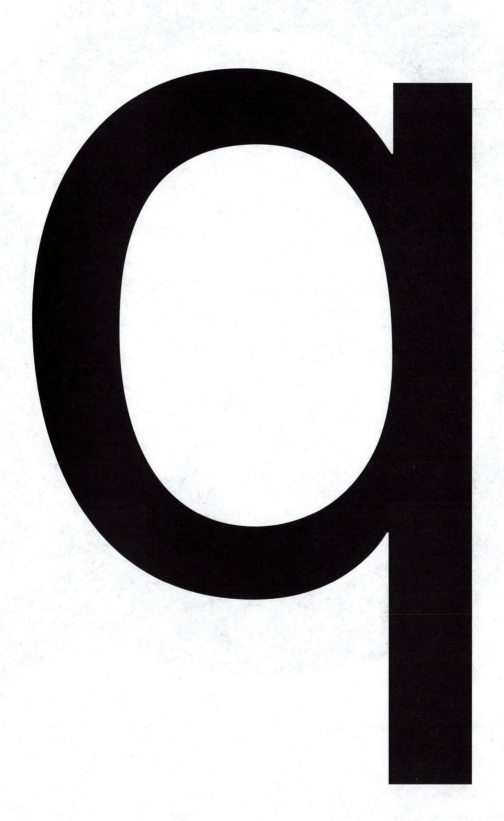

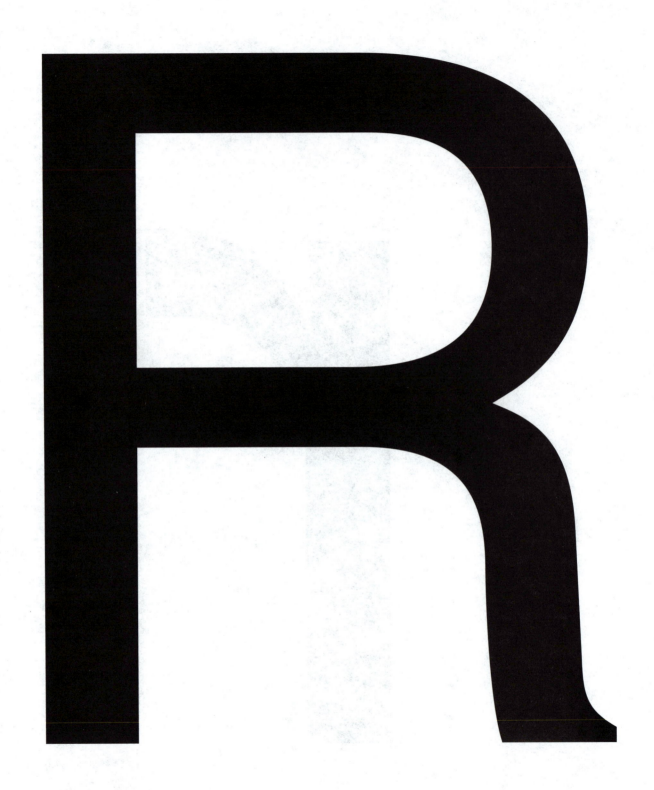

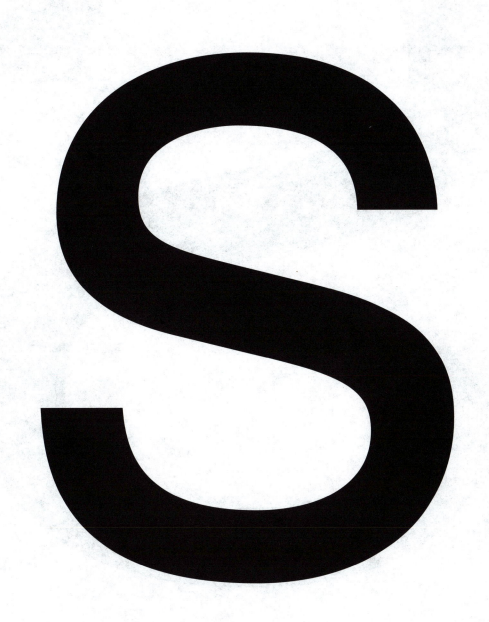

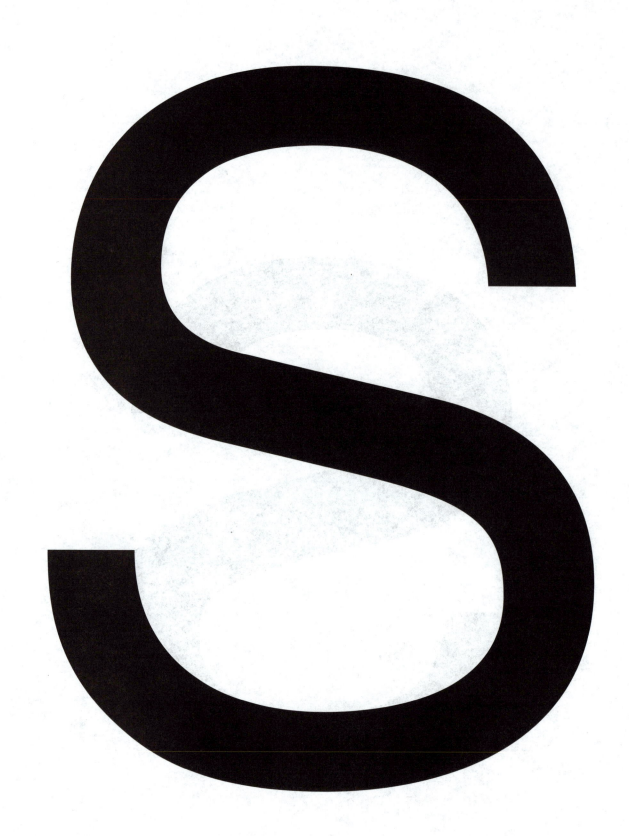

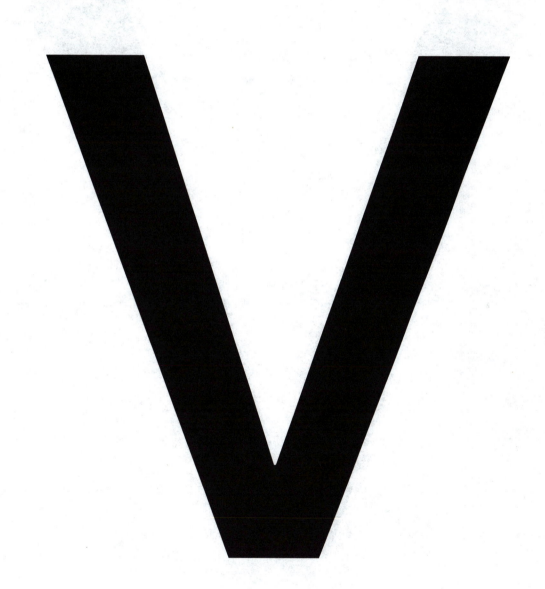

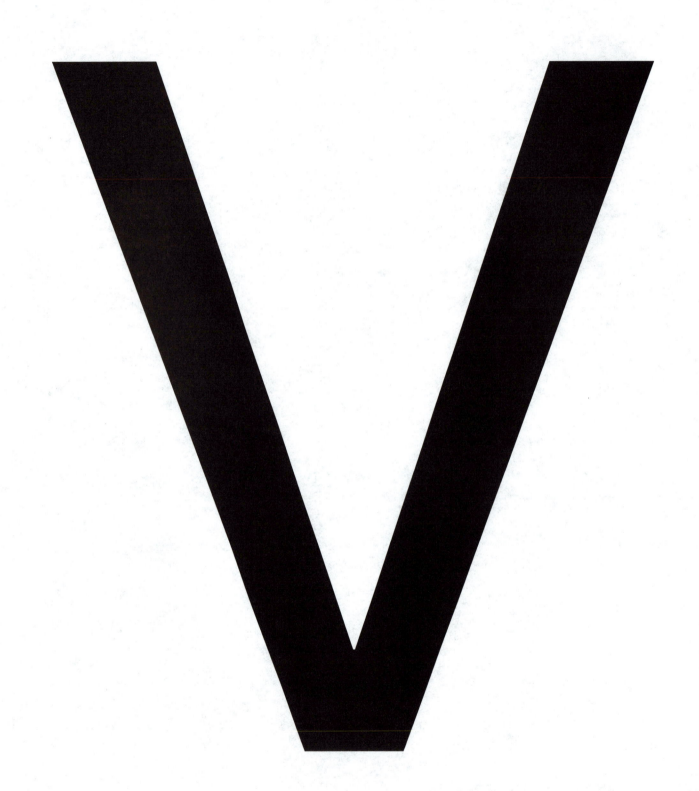

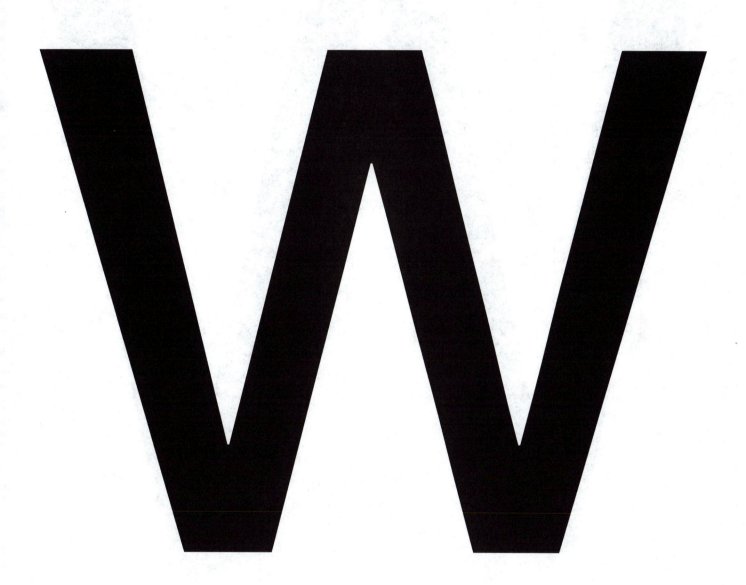

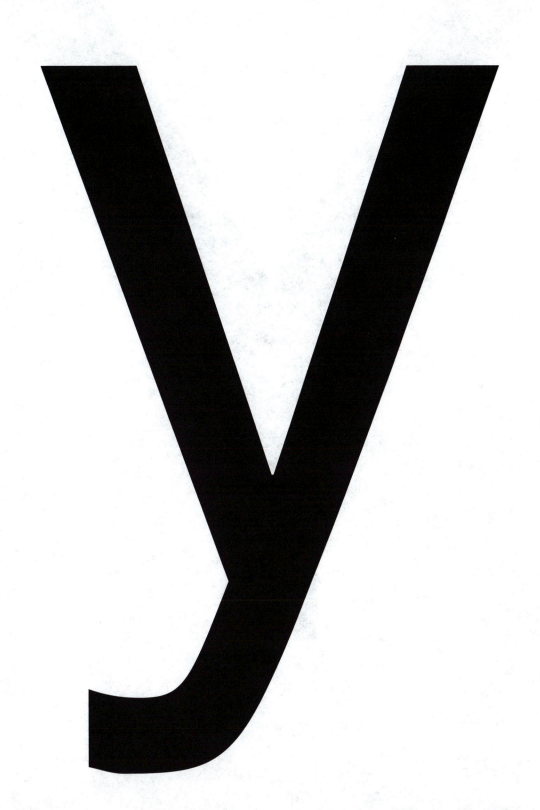

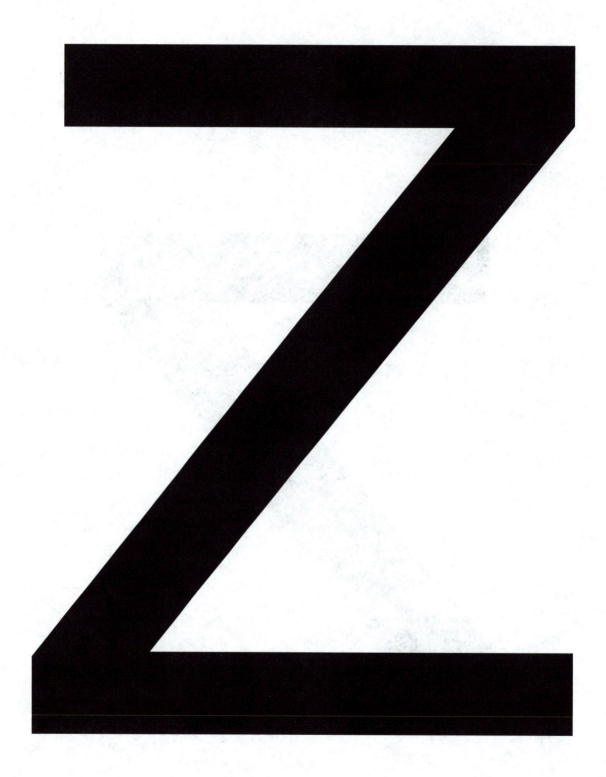